MW01296927

To Vicke Hepling — I enjoyed your Company at Unrigged 2019. Good luck in your Missouri Campaign!

Michael A. Serapino 3-30-21

Conned Conservatives and Led-on Liberals

Conned Conservatives
and
Led-on Liberals

You Think the Thoughts you think are yours?

Think Again!

Michael Anthony Serrapica

First Edition

ISBN: 9781728791241

Published by:

Performance Books

9123 Performance Ct.

Suite 3

Cresson, TX 76035

mas.pb@outlook.com

This book is dedicated to the open-minded, to those with the courage to admit when they are wrong. All others need not read it, they won't learn anything.

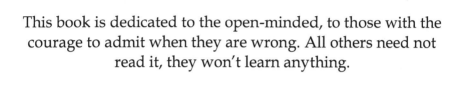

100% of all profits from the sale of this book are being donated to Represent.Us, the nation's largest grassroots anti-corruption campaign, bringing together conservatives and progressives to pass anti-corruption laws across the country.

Table of Contents

INTRODUCTION

On January 20, 2017 Donald J. Trump was sworn in as the forty-fifth President of the United States of America. Not long after, the host of the number-one show on the Fox News Channel, Bill O'Reilly was fired. What do these two occurrences have in common? Trump won his job and O'Reilly lost his for the same reason: Arrogance.

Both Trump and O'Reilly are well documented know-it-alls. In O'Reilly's case it was his downfall. Over the years (allegedly) he seems to have engaged in the sexual harassment of numerous female colleagues. True or not, the accusations were not his undoing, his hubris was. By refusing to own-up to any wrongdoing, when by all appearances there was something wrong, he lost trust. But more importantly, he lost advertisers for his show. The "bottom line" is what got Mr. O'Reilly the heave-ho.

In the case of Donald Trump, his arrogance actually helps him (with certain people) and it got him elected President. What's the difference?

During his campaign, Trump famously said he could go out and shoot someone without losing one vote. By all appearances, he was probably right. Not long after Trump's election, in a congressional runoff in Montana, the GOP candidate still won after beating up a reporter on the night before the election. Trump still won after calling the American people "stupid." Also, let's not forget "grab 'em by the pussy." So what's the difference?

Well, with both Donald Trump and the temperamental Republican in Montana, their followers had a stake in them because they promised these people things they want. But with Bill O'Reilly's audience it was no big loss. HOWEVER, there are much deeper, darker and more sinister reasons afoot, which most of us aren't even aware exist, let alone how they are used to manipulate our thoughts. That is why I decided to write this book.

I am just an average American (you know, one of you; those people President Trump thinks are "stupid"). There is an abundance of expert information out there from which we can learn how to protect ourselves from, let's say, the *phony sales pitch*. My goal was to learn how those who want my vote or my money (that includes taxes) or my allegiance, etc. work on my head to persuade me to trust them. As a non-expert, I did my study with no preconceived ideas or notions. The fact that I am your peer is what makes this book important to *you*. In the following pages I will share what I learned from the EXPERTS. There is no reason to blindly go along being conned or led-on.

On the day broadcasting icon Barbara Walters retired she appeared on Bill O'Reilly's FOX News Channel program *The O'Reilly Factor*. At one point in their conversation/interview O'Reilly commented on how he thought journalism, in America, has become different, especially on TV, adding that he now sees it as a means of promoting personal "agendas." Mr. O'Reilly hit the nail on the head. This book will explain WHY.

I am old enough to remember when Bill O'Reilly was a journalist for CBS and ABC television news, among others. This is not meant to imply that he no longer is. But his main function now, although not on the Fox News Channel (FNC) anymore, is to comment. Herein lays the problem. In America these days, prime-time television is crowded with ostensible reporters who are actually pontificators. There was a time when these types could only be found on hard-to-tune-in, AM radio stations. It is a problem because of the now prevalent desire for instant gratification and easy answers, due to the rise of technology. Mr. O'Reilly agrees, to the point of considering it "dangerous."

Let's not forget that before his downfall Bill O'Reilly was one of the most successful commentators on national television. That fact alone makes O'Reilly an expert in the art of persuasion; the ability to influence other people's thoughts. Actually, with that in mind, I decided to use one of his books as sort of a road map for this one. Not one of his novels, or "Killing So-and-So" series, but a book of the opinions that won him so many followers. The book was called *Pinheads and Patriots*.

I agree with some of Mr. O'Reilly's opinions and disagree with others. This is not to say I intend to debate his book point-by-point. However, I will question some of it. What I simply hope to do is present my own thoughts regarding how I feel as an American these days, like Mr. O'Reilly recommended in *his* book. My goal is to stimulate discussion among my fellow Americans regarding how we might help solve some of our problems.

There is nothing wrong with spirited, or even heated, debate as long as both sides get to state their case fairly. But certain members of Mr. O'Reilly's profession spout from a pulpit, as if delivering gospel. This *is dangerous!* Think about it: Don't we all know some people who are less than thoughtful and are easily sold a bill of goods? Let's call them "gullible." With the increasing reliance on electronic media, manipulation of the gullible is becoming easier than ever.

I might instead have titled this book *Plutocrats and Patriots.* I cannot say for sure if Mr. O'Reilly would agree with me one-hundred percent, but I think he does to a certain degree. In America these days, I see our country as having degenerated into a full blown plutocracy, in which we are being "governed" by the wealthy, and I am certainly not the first to propose this. These plutocrats are increasingly endeavoring to control the gullible through the unscrupulous, demagogue leaders of media and politics they invest in. But now that one of them has convinced enough of us to elect him President of the United States, the fight for equality might have become a fight for survival.

However, I do not feel we should fear all is lost. We the people of America have steered our country back on the right track before and we can again. Mr. O'Reilly agrees with me on this. To paraphrase him, the patriots outnumber the pinheads. Indeed. And the patriots also outnumber the plutocrats, somewhere in the neighborhood of "(The) 99%!"

Before beginning, I want to let you know just who I am that is asking you to take the time to read my views and consider what I say.

I am what Bill O'Reilly characterizes, in *Pinheads and Patriots*, as an ordinary American. Like him, and maybe like you, I come from working class folks. Unlike him, but probably like you, I do not have the benefit of a pulpit. However, as we all do, I have opinions that I hope might benefit others.

So here goes, this is me: I have a high school diploma (vocational) – that's it, no college. I have worked since the age of eleven, starting in my neighborhood drug store. I also loaded, and was a helper on, delivery trucks during high school. My first job after graduation was as a garage mechanic at a major department store. Okay, Sears, for five years. For the following thirty-three years, I was an aircraft mechanic, my vocation.

What makes a guy like "that" think he can write a book? Well, although I never attended formal college, I pride myself on the fact that I am a perpetual learner. I continually self-educate, by attending specialized schools and through personal study.

Like Bill O'Reilly, I have a background in broadcasting, although that career never took off as well for me. However, thanks to the skills and knowledge I attained, I did serve for several years as a media specialist for the union I belong to. In that position I did quite a lot of writing, and I learned that I like it. So I've worked hard to improve my proficiency at it. Additionally, I have had the encouragement of many who have read my work, as well as their compliments on being able to do it well, which is always motivating.

I am also a student (not an expert) of media and psychology. And I understand, as well as fear, the power of both to manipulate.

Primarily, I decided to write this book because I felt it was high time one of us "ordinary" Americans did. We are relentlessly bombarded by the views of professional opinion makers who are paid to make us believe what they want us to, or in some cases to make us believe what those who pay them want us to.

Therefore, one of "us" needed to do an examination of the views we are bombarded with, as well as the psychology of how we are made to believe them, and how we can defend ourselves from being led to act against our own best interests. And I hope to demonstrate that anyone can and should do what I did. One need not be an expert – one need only pay attention to them.

Through the research required for me to provide facts and evidence to substantiate my opinions and assertions, I was rewarded with a remarkable education. I gained invaluable knowledge about the science of persuasion and how it is used to manipulate those of us unaware as to how it works.

With my thanks and respect to you for taking an interest in my opinions and my newfound knowledge, I am excited to now share them. But please, keep in mind that my hope is not to make you change your mind or agree with me, for I have learned it's impossible to achieve either. My only hope is that when you read this book you will simply consider as well as discuss, like we all do every day with our fellow Americans, another point of view with an open mind. I have also learned that we can only change our own minds, and in order to do that – our minds must be *open*.

Sincerely, your fellow American,
Michael A. Serrapica

I

Discussing Definitions

Sticks and stones can break your bones but words can never harm you. That's what you think!

In *Pinheads and Patriots*, and on the air, Bill O'Reilly uses several well-worn terms and phrases to describe people and philosophies. His fellow commentators also apply many of these, as do the rest of us in everyday conversation. Researching these terms has shown me that certain ones, which most of us consider having straightforward meanings, are actually quite nuanced. They can have many meanings and carry different ones in different contexts.

What follows is not meant to be a lexicon, but a conversation about the *meaning of meanings.* My purpose in this exercise is to demonstrate that we ought to not take anything for granted. Most demagogues (And I am not hinting at anyone in particular – yet!) are clever wordsmiths. A term that has developed negative attributes, through thoughtful misuse, can make something innocent or good sound sinister or bad, and vice-versa.

If you look-up the terms below in the dictionary of your choice you will find, as I did, their actual meanings often have nothing to do with their perceived meanings. Some concepts we associate with patriotism can actually be subversive, and some we see as subversive can be patriotic. So here is my list of some popular terms I believe to deserve thought when heard or used, as opposed to being taken at face value.

Liberal: Often spoken with contempt by Conservatives, its actual dictionary meanings are: Favorable to or in accord with concepts of maximum individual freedom [something Conservatives also call for]; favorable to progress or reform [In other words: Willing to work to make things better.]; free from prejudice or bigotry, tolerant [The Golden Rule].

Progressive: Favoring or advocating progress, change, improvement, or reform, as opposed to wishing to maintain things as they are; employing or advocating more enlightened or *liberal* ideas. (Actually, liberal and progressive are synonyms, and they both also mean: Making progress toward better conditions.)

Conservative: Favoring the preservation of established customs, values, etc, and opposing innovation – disposed to preserve existing conditions, institutions, etc., or to restore traditional ones, and to limit change. (Taken literally, must this include change that is favorable to or in accord with concepts of maximum individual freedom because it is proposed by someone labeled Liberal?)

Independent: Not influenced or controlled by others in matters of opinion, conduct, etc.; thinking or acting for oneself: an independent thinker. *Politics*, a person who votes for candidates, measures, etc., in accordance with his or her own judgment and without regard to the endorsement of, or the positions taken by, any party. (Bill O'Reilly states the fact that he is a "registered Independent," as am I, in political affiliation. I think he would agree that he is a Right-leaning Independent, mostly siding with Conservatives, in point of view. I am admittedly a Left-leaning Independent, mostly siding with Liberals, in point of view. However, by definition, I believe most of us consider ourselves independent thinkers. Republicans, Democrats, Conservatives, Liberals, and Independents regularly cross Party lines when voting. Here we have an interesting example of nuance. Would you not agree?)

Democrat: An advocate of democracy. Democracy: A form of government in which the supreme power is vested in the people and exercised directly by them or by *their elected agents* under a free electoral system. Republican: An advocate of a republic. Republic: A state in which the supreme power rests in the body of citizens entitled to vote and is exercised by *representatives chosen* directly or indirectly *by them.* (All of the foregoing is pretty much interchangeable. Most of us have more in common than we sometimes remember. Focusing on that, as opposed to the differences, makes the pursuit of happiness a lot happier!)

Socialist and Communist: Here's where the nuances get really complicated. These two terms are often used interchangeably. In fact, some dictionaries simply use either one as the definition for the other. Actually, they have significant differences, and each has various types with subtle distinctions. Even scholars disagree about the meanings of each, as well as their understandings of the different forms of each. Both philosophies are mainly considered to have originated in the nineteenth century, but precursors such as Humanism date back to the eighteenth and speculation contends both might have origins going back to the early Stone Age.

Rather than examine the many forms of each, let us boil things down to the types that some of us seem to embrace or fear (depending on point of view) in America these days. You may find, as I did, some of the concepts we revile with the label of "socialism" are values held by American patriots. And some of the doctrines we are asked to accept as "patriotic" are actually subversive.

Many label former President Obama a Socialist. Fair enough, but if we consider the numerous types, we need to reasonably define which one. I feel the category he falls into is Social Democrat, which is one who advocates economic democracy (the people have a voice in economic policy) and social safety nets (programs designed to prevent the economically or physically vulnerable from falling into abject poverty).

In *Pinheads and Patriots*, Bill O'Reilly, referencing a series of debates on his TV show, opined that President Obama was not a "closet socialist" because he doesn't try to forcibly supervise the citizens' property, and socialists do. Actually, they don't. That's what Communists do.

Communists advocate that both capitalism and private ownership, regarding production or doing business, be done away with in order to establish a classless society. (World events have all but proven this to be unattainable.)

Socialists, on the other hand, assert that society benefits from capitalism, as long as it is governed by regulations. (I take this to mean that a duty of government is to protect society from any predatory abusers of capitalism.)

O'Reilly went on to say that Mr. Obama endorses certain socialist tenets, like "income redistribution" and "social justice" by-way-of legislation or executive orders. Let us analyze this by examining these two socialist tenets.

First: There are two types of income redistribution. Progressive, which is from the rich to the poor, and regressive, which is from the poor to the rich. Redistribution, of either type, has always been and will always be feverishly debated. Why? Because they are the fuses that ignite class warfare. The Haves want it all, the Have-Nots want enough. Since the administration that preceded Obama's favored regressive redistribution, and we let them get away with it, we the people are now in a war to get it back. With the election of Donald Trump, the tide of our war has once again turned against us.

Income redistribution can be achieved in several ways. The easiest one is probably taxation. One night, I was watching *The O'Reilly Factor*. Bill and his (then) FNC colleague Lou Dobbs were having a discussion about taxes. They agreed that we all need to pay our fair share. An example of unfair taxation was talked about, i.e., some corporations pay *none*, and GE was singled out. They also discussed President Obama's appointing of, GE CEO and Board Chairman, Jeffrey Immelt to the President's Economic Recovery Advisory Board. (To avoid digression, we will save him for later.)

One question we should ask here is: If O'Reilly and Dobbs and you and I agree there are some crooks not pulling their weight, and it can be corrected by income redistribution through fair taxation, who cares if it's a socialist tenet? Another question is: Judging by his friends, did President Obama agree with us? I feel he did, but was somewhat hindered because of his obligations. (Again, not to digress, we will work on that later, too.)

Let us move on to the second tenet, social justice. It is grounded upon the principle of equality, the value of human rights, and recognizes the dignity of every human being. It is based upon the teachings of Saint Thomas Aquinas. It is also cited in our Declaration of Independence: "We hold these truths to be self-evident, that all men are created equal, that they are endowed by their Creator with certain unalienable Rights, that among these are Life, Liberty and the pursuit of Happiness." Again, who cares if it's also a socialist tenet? It's another common value. That's good, isn't it?

Finally, there is one more thought provoking difference between Socialism and Communism. Socialism generally aims to have as many people as possible influence how the economy works. (Think: Republic and Democracy.) Communism seeks to concentrate that number into a smaller amount. (Think: Plutocracy, Kleptocracy, Oligarchy, and the popular, Conservative catchphrase "Small Government".)

II

Alternative Facts

There are three sides to every story, ours, theirs, and the truth.

Let us continue our exercise of taking a hard look at what we hear and what might motivate those we hear it from. As opposed to accepting "facts" automatically, as offered by the first source we get them from, it is safer to be skeptical, even if (maybe especially if [?]) that source claims to side with our personal ideology. Examining just a couple of issues will illustrate the importance of a little judicious questioning.

Example # 1: Tea Party Theatrics

Glenn Beck and Sarah Palin are given credit, by some, for being "leaders" of the Tea Party movement. In *Pinheads and Patriots*, Bill O'Reilly said they "blasted" the Tea Party into national prominence. Is this impression the truth, or is it just their side? The facts are easy enough to verify.

January 24, 2009: A demonstration took place, referred to as a "Tea Party" protest. It was organized by one Trevor Leach, chairman of the Young Americans for Liberty in New York State, to protest runaway spending and taxes they felt were "unfair."

February 16, 2009: Tea Party members, as well as reports by the *New York Times*, *The Atlantic*, and *NPR* credited a conservative activist named Keli Carender with organizing the first, according to the Tea Party – "one of the first" according to the news agencies, Tea Party, although the term was not used at the time.

February 19, 2009: During a broadcast from the floor of the Chicago Mercantile Exchange, CNBC reporter Rick Santelli was described to have "ranted" on-air that President Obama's Homeowners Affordability and Stability Plan would be "subsidizing losers' mortgages." He went on to suggest a "Chicago Tea Party" to protest. His televised tirade, more than any other event, is cited for the Tea Party movement being "blasted" into national prominence.

March 13, 2009: Glenn Beck proposed the 9/12 Project on his TV broadcast to promote "9 principles and 12 values" (he believes were) held by our country's Founding Fathers. Some members of the Tea Party are also 9/12ers.

September 12, 2009: Beck "endorsed" the Taxpayer March on Washington, a Tea Party protest.

February 6, 2010: Sarah Palin was the keynote speaker at the inaugural Tea Party convention in Nashville, Tennessee. She was criticized for accepting a fee, reported to have been $100,000. Tea Party organizers were also criticized for offering it. (A *New York Times* article stated that the amount could not be verified.)

August 28, 2010: Beck hosted a "Restoring Honor" rally in Washington D.C. in front of The Lincoln Memorial on the anniversary of Dr. Martin Luther King Jr.'s "I Have a Dream" speech, which was given at the same location. Beck received wide criticism for his choice of date and place. Tea Party members may have attended, but it was not advertised as a Tea Party event.

October 2010: The *Washington Post* conducted a poll of 647 local Tea Party organizers, asking them: "Which national figure best represents your groups?" Thirty four percent said "no one," fourteen percent said "Sarah Palin" and seven percent said "Glenn Beck."

Additionally, here is a very-little-known fact: Before all of the above events took place, the "grassroots" Tea Party movement was initially created by plutocrats! Citizens for a Sound Economy (CSE) was founded in 1984 by Charles and David Koch of Koch Industries, a.k.a. The Koch Brothers (Draffan, George /2000/ The Corporate Consensus: A Guide to the Institutions of Global Power). CSE started the Tea Party in 2002 (usteaparty.com).

What's the bottom line? The facts demonstrate that, chronologically, the tea was brewing long before Beck or Palin arrived at the party. As for Santelli, although I think he was an insensitive louse for calling people who were fleeced by shifty mortgage brokers "losers," his comments did the most to energize the Tea Party.

The appropriate conclusion is that Beck and Palin, rather than being "leaders," simply capitalized on opportunity. Their preaching appeals to some in the Tea Party. Because of that, some of the Tea Party (14% in Palin's case and 7% in Beck's) apparently gravitated toward them. The Tea Party helped to blast *them* into the public forefront, not the other way around.

Example # 2: The Fox Hunt

In the fall of 2009, the White House "declared war" on the Fox News Channel. On Sunday, September 20, President Obama refused to appear on FNC's *Fox News Sunday* with Chris Wallace, while attending the equivalent interview programs of all the other, major networks. At first, the administration cited an FNC decision to not air a prior Obama, prime time appearance. Subsequently, they said it was due to the manner in which FNC covered the administration. They called FNC "a wing of the Republican Party." Wallace, of *Fox News Sunday*, called White House officials "crybabies." The war (of words) went on.

Then, on October 22, the Obama administration tried to exclude FNC from official interviews with, Treasury Department Official, Kenneth Feinberg. Every other network refused to participate unless their sister organization was included. They expressed the opinion that the administration had crossed a line by excluding any specific news agency. The White House backed down and the "war" soon ended.

Any logical person ought to be puzzled by those actions by the White House. Every administration probably engages in forms of censorship, out of necessity. If news might threaten lives or derail important policy it must be withheld until it will not. A perfect example was the raid on Osama Bin Laden's compound in Pakistan. But the omission of a legitimate news agency (which FNC undeniably is), because you don't like their editorial stance, is the kind of censorship one would expect from a tyranny, not from an administration widely considered Liberal.

The reason I include this episode is because I was disappointed by the fact that Bill O'Reilly failed to mention the defense of FOX, by all of its sister organizations, in his discussion of the White House "war." On pages 32 – 39 of *Pinheads and Patriots*, he referred to "the war of words" and "the ratings war." He described how the White House's rhetoric boosted Fox's ratings, and how long it took for him to get his autographed picture of President Obama.

O'Reilly titled his essay "The Great Ratings War." Virtually all of his discussion was about the other news agencies and it was virtually all negative, making references to the Left as "crazy" and "kooky," although he regularly denounces name-calling. He also bragged about how FOX is reportedly watched and trusted more than all the other TV news outlets. Good for FOX, but show some appreciation!

The point is this: Anyone not familiar with the aforementioned incidents from the fall of 2009, and having read only O'Reilly's account, would be led to believe that not only was FOX in a "war" with the White House but also with the other news agencies. As far as ratings go they were and always will be. If Mr. O'Reilly had only talked about ratings, in a statistical sense, he would have been fine. However, as soon as he opened the door regarding the dispute with the White House he had a responsibility to tell the whole story. Including the fact that FOX was defended by all of its sister organizations. One can only speculate as to why he did not.

Perhaps he found it difficult to thank those "crazy, kooky" Lefties? Whatever the reason, being aware of the episode with the White House, I felt let down by his poor retelling of it. Additionally, continuing our theme of questioning facts, I submit this as an example of fact *revision* through fact *omission*.

Finally, here is another FACT to question: President Trump regularly bans or refuses to cooperate with media outlets he disfavors or, more likely, fears. Why aren't FNC and other Trump favored news outlets refusing to cooperate with him in defense of their sister organizations, now that the shoe is on the other foot?

III

No Spin? No Way!

"You can fool all the people some of the time, and some of the people all the time, but you cannot fool all the people all the time." Abraham Lincoln

Spin: "A particular bias, interpretation, or point of view, intended to create a favorable [or sometimes, unfavorable] impression when presented to the public." *(Oxford, U.S. English Dictionary)*

The preceding chapter examined two examples of how facts can be perceived differently, depending on one's bias, interpretation or point of view, i.e., spin. Since we each have our own personal outlook, virtually everything is open to debate.

Bill O'Reilly used to open his nightly TV program by exclaiming: "CAUTION: You are about to enter the no spin zone!" (CAUTION: Not necessarily!)

Example: On his show one night, O'Reilly did a segment about a recent "sting" of a PBS executive by a bunch of conservative college kids who try to discredit liberals. While secretly videotaping their meeting, they baited the man into making indiscrete statements. O'Reilly's segment was ostensibly about whether this ought to be considered a prank or true undercover journalism. His two guests remained pretty much on point. But Bill kept referring to (his perception of) the PBS mentality, which was not the issue. The fact that he thinks "everyone" at PBS is a Left leaning, Left thinking, Left handed, Leftist Lefty was all he talked about. That's not spin?

No matter what they say, FOX News has a palpable conservative bias. It is easily observable. Much of their reporting, and practically all of their commentary, tries to spin the audience toward their slant and away from what they perceive is the competition's slant. Of course, whether intentional or not, everyone does. But I think most of what FOX aloofly refers to as "the mainstream media" (generally) tries to uphold the time-honored, journalistic standard of remaining unbiased, for the most part. (If you read Bernard Goldberg's book *Bias* you will understand why I say "for the most part.") They (usually) don't *root* (blatantly, anyway). But to hear the FNC blowhards tell it, all other media except their beloved provider are Leftists. That's not spin?

When I studied sports-casting, thirty-five years ago, I was taught that it is improper to root for either team. The on field events ought to be reported as they occur. It is okay to be colorful and excited, i.e., entertaining. However, not in any way that is biased toward one side or the other.

In America these days, we see and hear rooting in many places where it does not belong. Sports-casting is probably the only media venue where it remains absent (well, for the most part). The spin is everywhere!

The important thing to keep in mind about the spin is that it is a point of view. Taken as such, and scrutinized for what it's worth and who it comes from, helps keep things in true perspective. Anyone capable of doing that has no need to fear a demagogue. I am more fearful of the gullible.

Bill O'Reilly opined in *Pinheads and Patriots* that the American people seem to be losing the ability to scrutinize, which makes us more vulnerable to manipulation by charismatic, phony politicians that only want power. (OH, HOW RIGHT HE WAS!) He attributes this to the increasing reliance on machines to do our thinking for us. I totally agree, and see it already happening.

America is turning into a modern-day Cargo Cult. Citizens act like the "unsophisticated" (depending on one's interpretation of the nuances in the meaning of "sophistication") Polynesian, native inhabitants of Allied occupied Pacific islands during World War II. They worshipped the C-47 (military version of the Douglas DC-3) cargo planes as gods, dropping gifts from heaven (hence the name, "Cargo Cult"). Today, we wait for the gods at Apple Corporation to drop the next electronic panacea. The danger is the inclination to become reliant on it. My dear, departed mother used to say: "The less you do, the less you want to do." As usual – mom was right – and the less you *think* the less you want to *think!*

The way all this relates to the spin is that, no matter how unintentional it may be, everyone has a bias. In itself that is not bad, it is just a fact of human nature. What is bad is the promotion of one's bias as fact. What is worse is accepting someone else's bias without thinking.

Psychiatrist Mark Goulston, in his book *Just Listen*, discusses how our brains are wired to jump to conclusions: "Instinct" uses past experience to make quick decisions, for the ultimate purpose of protecting us from harm. Demagogues take advantage of this by addressing our base instincts and fears. What is the solution? Dr. Goulston says: "Think about what you're thinking." Take a step back and weigh your *perceptions* against *reality*.

Several years ago, I saw TV's "Judge Judy" interviewed by Larry King. He asked her about how she analyzes evidence in order to reach a verdict. Since only one side is telling the truth, but both sides "swear to tell the truth," how does she reach a conclusion she can live with? Her answer stuck with me and I use it as helpful advice. She said that she simply asks herself: "What makes the most sense?" Basically, she puts herself in the other persons' shoes and considers whether she would do what they claim, given the same circumstances. By determining whoever sounded the most reasonable, she comes to a conclusion.

Let's use Judge Judy's method to examine Bill O'Reilly's PBS remarks. Is it reasonable to claim that "everyone" at PBS is a Leftist? Additionally, what difference does it make?

When I hear a Conservative (sorry, Right-leaning Independent) like Bill O'Reilly make such a big deal about his belief that certain entities have Liberal or Leftist tendencies, I ask myself: Why? Is it to infer they don't have a right to? Is it to insinuate that leaning Left is wrong or bad? Let me state this clearly: I do not consider Mr. O'Reilly to be a demagogue. Pompous? Yes, but not a demagogue. I think he tries to be helpful and sensible. He just does it from a perspective that could be a bit more tolerant of those he disagrees with, which is (actually) what a lot of us do.

However, we do have certain dangerous demagogues in media and politics. And whether it is a sincere Conservative or an insincere demagogue talking, those on the Right almost always try to make the Left sound undesirable. It might be with a raised brow, or roll of the eyes, or sarcastically pronouncing Left or Liberal through a condescending sneer. That is spin. When I put myself in their shoes, like Judge Judy, the conclusion I come up with is that they are (rather heavy-handedly and obviously, I might add) trying to discredit those who oppose their political beliefs.

In the case of PBS, my conclusions are: (1) "Everyone" there is probably not a Lefty, and (2) it doesn't make a difference. Since this is (still) America, we all have a right to our individual beliefs. It's fine to disagree, but wrong to insinuate that those who do are fundamentally troublesome. As long as Big Bird keeps teaching kids how to read, write and count – and as long as I get documentaries that I am entertained by and can learn from – I don't care how the employees at PBS vote. I also don't care how those who work at FOX vote. (Actually, I care more about how we "don't vote." We will get into that more deeply as we move on.)

Finally, some observations regarding political spin: In virtually every case, when so-called Liberal commentators attack Conservative issues, it is the issues they attack. Conservative commentators, more often than not, seem to prefer attacking Liberals personally, just for being Liberals.

Maybe you're thinking I am wrong about everything I have said? Maybe you're right? What's important, and what I'm trying to encourage, is that you *think about what you're thinking!*

And *finally*, finally – a footnote: I learned something else from watching Bill O'Reilly that warrants adding here – the difference between spin and outright sham.

The Reverend Al Sharpton used to have a show on MSNBC. Of course his bias was Liberal and he spent a lot of time trying to discredit Conservatives, particularly those employed by FNC. On one broadcast of *The O'Reilly Factor*, Bill did a report about three separate instances where Sharpton denounced Mr. O'Reilly for certain things he said. The problem was that he never said them.

O'Reilly first played the video segments, of what he "said," as shown on Sharpton's program, and the Reverend's denunciations of Bill for saying them. O'Reilly then played the same clips *in their entirety*. What Bill demonstrated, superbly, was the difference between spin, which is the endeavor to get others to lean toward your cause, and sham, which is outright lying – PERIOD!

By taking selective words out of context, Rev. Sharpton changed Mr. O'Reilly's intended meaning completely. That is fraud. It not only does disservice to the intended victim, but also to those who the Reverend might have spun to his own side. Worst of all, it does disservice to (Rev. Al Sharpton) the perpetrator, by utterly destroying his credibility.

O'Reilly had two guests on, and they discussed Sharpton's sham. The point was made that Rev. Al might not have even been aware of the butchering of O'Reilly's words. In fairness to Rev. Sharpton, I (personally) failed to follow up with his show to find out if he ever made amends. But whether or not an apology was given, someone was fired, or policies were changed, I need to thank the Rev. Al Sharpton. Because this episode exemplifies and validates my advice, at the beginning of the previous chapter, about "facts": As opposed to accepting "facts" automatically, as offered by the first source we get them from, it is safer to be skeptical – even if (maybe especially if [?]) that source proclaims to side with our personal ideology.

IV

Propaganda and Spin: The Techniques of Tyranny

"If you tell a lie big enough and keep repeating it, people will eventually come to believe it." Joseph Goebbels

Spin is a science. When used to achieve a calculated purpose, be that to entice customers to buy one's product or convince voters that one's politics are better, it is no accident.

Propaganda and spin are not exactly synonymous but they are closely related. While spin is a particular bias, propaganda refers to the methods of spreading that bias. They are both deeply rooted in Social Psychology, and propagandists or "spinmeisters" study it, to hone the art of persuasion. Large entities like corporations, news media and political parties will actually employ cadres of social psychologists. The subject is truly fascinating and well worth further study when you have the time.

As with Socialism and Communism, propaganda has many forms. By learning to recognize some of the common types, we can arm ourselves against those who attempt to sway us (in the wrong direction) if we remain ignorant.

First off, all propaganda is not inherently bad. It can be intended to help or harm. Some examples of positive propaganda are public service campaigns encouraging us to quit smoking, report crime, get a mammogram or donate to charity. These and all other types of initiatives meant to advertise a thing or point of view can be correctly defined as propaganda. However, today the term is avoided when describing positive propaganda. This trend developed around World War II, due mainly to Hitler's relentless and destructive use of negative propaganda. Since then, propaganda as a device, as well as the word itself, is almost exclusively thought of negatively.

Now, let's familiarize ourselves with a few of the prevalent techniques of propaganda, which are used to spread the spin:

Ad hominem: (Latin) To attack one's opponents instead of their arguments. Example: Bill O'Reilly referring to the *New Yorker* magazine as the "crazy Left" *New Yorker* magazine. (This is also an example of Labeling or Name-calling.)

Ad nauseam: The relentless repetition of an idea or slogan. Example: "Fox News is Fair and Balanced," indirectly suggesting that everyone else is somehow not.

Appeal to fear and Appeal to prejudice: Exactly what they say. These techniques try to manipulate the audience by addressing their base instincts. The propagandist tries to make his listeners feel they should be anxious or even panicked (fear) *unless* – or tries to make them feel they will be better than certain others (prejudice) *if* – they follow his advice. Example: Donald Trump's assertions that certain ethnicities or religions, en masse, are dangerous to America.

Disinformation: Falsification of public records with the intention of creating support for a cause. Example: The claim that Iraq was developing "weapons of mass destruction," in order to justify going to war, when in fact they were not.

Labeling and/or Name-calling: Labeling can be used to either make the subject look more attractive with euphemisms, example: "Pro-Life," which is used by Anti-Abortionists to infer that anyone who disagrees with them is pro-death – or unattractive with dysphemisms, example: "Pro-Abortion" to describe those who are Pro-Choice, insinuating that they favor baby killing. Name-calling is similar but exclusively negative.

Flag Waving: To appeal to an audience by making them believe that supporting the propagandist will make them more patriotic. Example: The phrase "War on Terror." With these three short words it is implied that national security will be served by a continuous state of war.

Lying and Deception: All of the above can be based upon outright Lying and often are. Deception can include half-truths, white-lies, and obfuscation.

These represent just a few methods. Looking into the many, various types reveals a striking commonality: They all appeal to our *emotions* as opposed to our *intellect*.

V

Ideas about Ideas

Think About What You're Thinking!

As Bill O'Reilly points out on page forty-seven of *Pinheads and Patriots*, we Americans are an emotional people. Whether Liberal or Conservative we are passionate. We have strong convictions. We have conscientious patriotic and moral values. For these very reasons, we need to take a hard look at the information we are fed.

Because we maintain strong emotional ties to our beliefs, and because propaganda tactics appeal to our emotions, propagandists use our own ideas to win our trust. Often that trust is in their best interest and not ours.

We Americans are also argumentative. We enjoy discussion and debate. We like defending our ideas to those who disagree with us, hoping to win their endorsement or at least get them to see our side.

With that in mind, I want to now present some popular topics of discussion. These ideas are often debated in everyday conversation, as well as the greater, public forums of politics and media. They are also ammunition for demagogues because of the emotional reactions they evoke.

My goal is to stimulate our thinking, not win any arguments. And by *stimulate* I mean (to) encourage the scrutiny of our personal ideas regarding these topics. In other words, to get us thinking about what we're thinking. By doing so, we might identify the emotional currency they hold for demagogues.

Since there is really no particular order of importance, I will just list them alphabetically.

Abortion

This issue has gotten people killed, and I'm not referring to the unborn. The ongoing debate not only encompasses its morality, but also whether or not it deserves any government funding (Planned Parenthood). Anti-abortionists refer to themselves as "Pro-Life" and call those who are Pro-Choice "Pro-Abortion."

I believe it is safe to say that anyone who kills another human being for having, or performing, an abortion is insane. It would be equally insane for someone to proclaim them self "Pro-Abortion." However, being Pro-Choice is something else entirely. (I said I wouldn't try to win any arguments!)

Abortions were performed before they were legalized, and will continue to be even if they are re-criminalized. Legalized abortion simply protects those who need to terminate a pregnancy, for whatever reason, with the ability to ensure it is done safely. Being Pro-Choice only means that one respects the right of another to choose abortion as an alternative. Whether or not one respects that right, others will occasionally choose it.   Government funding ensures that anyone in need of an abortion can have it. Like any other healthcare issue, in a humane society, it is that society's duty to provide it. (Of course, this is my opinion. Healthcare, and especially *Universal* Healthcare, is another topic of contention.)

Abortion's morality is a double-edged sword. Anti-abortionists feel any abortion is immoral. But abortions are done for moral reasons all the time.

So how do demagogues take advantage of all this? No Republican who is Pro-Choice has, or ever will, won the party's nomination for President. That is because Republicans know their conservative base is staunchly Anti-Abortion. Furthermore, they must characterize any Pro-Choice, political opponent as a godless, "Pro-Abortion," baby-killer.

The saddest part is that many Anti-Abortion voters consider this the only issue that matters.

By nature, no Pro-Choice arguments can be considered demagogic, because they defend freedom of choice. Those who are Anti-Abortion (Anti-Choice) will always say it is not their choice to make. Nevertheless, if put in that position, they too will be compelled to make a choice – one way or another. Either choice will have life-long repercussions.

What is the easiest way to keep from becoming emotionally vulnerable to propaganda that targets abortion? Do what I do: I keep in mind that, whether legal or illegal, abortions will be performed. I am thankful and relieved at not having to make the choice. And regarding those who are forced to make the difficult decision, I wish them luck and I mind my own business.

Big Government

Is this idea a valid concept or just a catch-phrase? I think it's a little of both. Republican, Presidential candidate Wendell Willkie is credited with using the term in 1940, as a play-on-words against the expression "Big Business." His intention was to indicate that a "Big Government," i.e., one with the power to intervene, was needed to "combat corporate tyranny." Today, the term Big Government is used by (so-called) Conservatives and free (meaning *regulation free*) trade advocates to ridicule government that sticks its big nose in where it is not wanted. (Republican values have certainly changed!)

The diametrical idea, "Small Government," is used to describe the type of government that is desired by free traders, one that minds its own business. Proponents of Small Government believe government should only be involved in issues of national interest (foreign policy), defense, and the law. Everything else is to be left up to the individual.

What we, those "in the middle," need to ask ourselves are: What contradictions are contained within these opposing ideas? And: How do they affect our individual freedoms and self-interests?

As stated, I think Big Government (and Small Government) is, at the same time, a valid concept and a catch-phrase. When used as an abbreviated way to describe a type of government that is granted the authority to fulfill its duty of protecting individual rights, it is a valid concept. That is how Wendell Willkie meant it. But in America these days, it has become a plutocrat catch-phrase.

Through demagogue politicians and media pundits, many of us have been led to believe that Big Government is a bad thing, which hinders our freedom of choice. They promote Small Government as the way to go, because it limits interference in private matters. By examining the facts, we can easily see the contradictions in this.

When we elect a government, any government, it is for the sole purpose of protecting our property. That includes not only real property, but intellectual and emotional property as well, i.e., "Life, Health, Liberty or Possessions." This idea was first proposed by Scottish philosopher John Locke in the seventeenth century and was endorsed by our Founding Fathers in the Declaration of Independence: "Life, Liberty and the pursuit of Happiness." The goal was, and still is, to protect those rights to property for all citizens, not just a few with financial influence and the psychotic desire to possess *all* property. When the avaricious ridicule *effective* government as "Big Government" it is simply word-play, to convince us that their interests are commensurate with our interests.

Republican and former Presidential candidate, Patrick J. Buchanan has spoken out extensively about the special interests that have infiltrated and are destroying his beloved G.O.P. I disagree philosophically with many of Mr. Buchanan's beliefs, but I emphatically agree that he is brilliant and loves America. In his book, *Where the Right Went Wrong* (which I highly recommend), he talks about how "Corporate America" is the piggy-bank of the G.O.P. but its philosophy has changed. American corporations used to see the value of protecting the American economy. Now America can be damned!

Global American companies now want, expect and get tremendous tax incentives, government subsidies, authorization to bring foreign workers here because they can pay them less, free-rein to send their manufacturing plants and jobs outside U.S. borders and the freedom to import their own products back here without tariffs to be sold to American citizens, as credit for their contributions to our elected representatives.

I would add to that: They have also been doing a good job of convincing many American workers to believe this subversive behavior is in their best interest.

Nevertheless, hope is beginning to shine. Pat Buchanan wrote *Where the Right Went Wrong* in 2004. Now, thanks to their insatiable greed, the ravenous radicals he described are beginning to go a bit too far.

More Americans are starting to realize that "Big" and "Small" Government have become nothing more than propaganda labels. And that the more regulative power our government relinquishes the less it can effectively protect the rights of the many from the wants of the few. But what can we do about it?

John Locke advised that the people shall be the ultimate judges of whether the government is working in their best interest. (Remember, that means all the people, including those who make up the government.) Locke added that when it is determined said government is not, then the governed shall have the right to "legitimate revolution." Luckily for us, the Founding Fathers gave us the ability to have bloodless revolutions, we call these free elections.

However, this brings up another, present-day problem. If, as is becoming more and more apparent, politicians from both major parties are indentured to plutocrats, who do we elect? The reason I ask this question is because no candidate has ever been elected President unless he was aligned with either of the major parties. It is also widely believed that none ever will be. If the next election we vote in is to be truly *revolutionary* I think we have reached a point where this logic needs to be re-evaluated.

Entitlement

The idea of Entitlement has been a historical sore spot for some Americans who feel they are entitled to be greedy. Irrespective of the separation of church and state, so-called Conservative politicians perpetually run on platforms which ostensibly embrace Judeo-Christian values. However, the value of charity does not seem to count.

Now, more than ever before, the Right Wing's attacks on Entitlement programs have become uncharitably aggressive. They use the word "entitlement" as a synonym for "handout." This is outright, deceptive propaganda. The truth is an Entitlement is exactly that, something we are *entitled* to. It is neither charity nor a handout. It is insurance, funded by our taxes, which we are entitled to collect when necessary.

I have been unemployed a couple of times, and have collected Unemployment insurance thanks to the fact that I must pay for it when employed. I am grateful that I have never needed Welfare or food stamps, but I appreciate their availability as well as my own ability to fund them, "just in case!" But many of us, with the mindset of "that will never happen to me," have been taken in by the rhetoric that an Entitlement is a handout to "freeloaders." Recent events started to unravel this plutocrat scam.

Thanks to the criminal mismanagement of our economy by self-indulgent plutocrats, unemployment exploded. Moreover, those needing Unemployment insurance included a great number of workers who lost high-paying, white-collar jobs. Do you think at least some of them might have thought "that will never happen to me"? What about the uproar over the proposed abrogation of Medicare and Social Security? All of us fund these two Entitlement programs with every paycheck and none of us think "that will never happen to me." We all desire, deserve and *pay* for them.

Are there freeloaders taking unfair advantage of certain Entitlement programs? Of course, but you don't throw out the baby with the bath water! The hard part is to weed out the freeloaders from them, in order to keep them intact for those who have earned them. This is hard because it requires these programs to be governed through diligent "regulation," a word that is abhorrent to plutocrats and the piggish politicians in their employ.

I attended a lecture some years ago, given by a man named Rick Steves. You might know who he is. He has created a nice business from his love of travel. He writes and sells books, also sells merchandise, and produces travel shows for PBS. Europe is his stated, favorite travel destination. One topic he discussed at his lecture was taxes. In Europe, he informed us, citizens pay taxes that are notably higher than ours. However, in return they expect and receive benefits to which their entitlement is unquestioned.

We Americans, on the other hand, will reflexively vote for any candidate who promises to cut taxes. But at the same time we expect to get what we are entitled to. The logic seems to be that it's an Entitlement when we need it, but it's a handout when the other guy does. To top it off, we don't want to pay for any of it!

Was the bailout of bankers, who fleeced America, an Entitlement or a hand-out? Would that money not have been better used to bail out their victims? And, after having witnessed the bankers' crime and the government's coddling, many of us still say: "Don't raise taxes on the corporations or the wealthy, because it will raise mine too!"

Those of us "in the middle" need to (figuratively) "come to Jesus" and accept the fact that we cannot have it both ways. We will always pay taxes and we will always be entitled to services in return. What we must do is demand that our representatives (literally) "pull their finger out," as the British like to say, and regulate our Entitlement programs fairly. Additionally, in order to protect what we are entitled to, we must demand they collect taxes from *all* Americans fairly.

France

These days, most Americans have sympathy, some even admiration, for France. After watching France endure a string of horrifying terrorist attacks, survive them and keep progressing, many of us have displayed the French flag (usually on *Facebook*). But not too many years ago, France and the USA had a rift. Many Americans considered the French laughable, even cowardly, because they had the courage to tell us we were wrong. A lot of us lacked the courage to listen and learn.

No, I am not French. However, I appreciate the fact that if there were no France there would be no America. Benjamin Franklin begged them to help us in our revolt against the British. They did and, of course, we won. If they had not, it is virtually certain that we would have lost.

The aforementioned rift came about when France opposed the Bush Administration's decision to go to war with Iraq. France was by no means the only country to do so. They were, however, the most vocal and they took a stand. But instead of defending their right to disagree, our Administration chose France as a patsy, to ridicule in the media, deflecting the heat away from them. Example: The re-naming of French fries to "Freedom fries" (flag-waving and indirect or reverse, name-calling propaganda) in the United States House of Representatives' cafeteria, at the direction of two Republican Congressmen.

As things turned out, France, and every other country that opposed invading Iraq, was right. It has now, finally and unfortunately, become evident that the only thing the invasion of Iraq by the United States did was destabilize the region.

I used to work with a retired Marine sergeant. He told me a story about a time when he and several of his younger charges were on leave in France. They were in a bar and his young Marines, being young Marines, wanted to prove how tough they were by "engaging" a similar sized group of military men from another country. When the older, more experienced sergeant realized what was about to happen he intervened to determine whether he should let his men "have fun" or if they might be getting in over their heads. When he learned from the other group that they were French legionnaires he immediately told his men to cut it out, and pack up to leave. They protested that they were MARINES! The sergeant basically told them that if they wanted to stay "conscious" Marines they had better not try to mix it up with legionnaires.

My friend the sergeant appreciated not only what the French are capable of, but also what they withstood. True, World Wars I and II were ultimately won thanks to U.S. involvement. But we didn't fight them on our soil, the French did. He knew, too, that it took courage, not cowardice, for France to speak out against the Bush Government's needless war, perhaps more courage than it takes to endure physical attacks.

By mocking a country that has been our friend and ally since before we were a sovereign nation simply because they criticize us (justifiably) we make ourselves look like arrogant, unappreciative fools. The Bush Administration didn't care about looking arrogant or unappreciative, because they were. They also had sinister motives for mocking France. The rest of us Americans do not. We are in their debt. The above lesson is: Don't be a "fair-weather-friend." If you want to dish it out, learn how to take it!

Freedom of Religion

On pages 110 – 113 of *Pinheads and Patriots*, Bill O'Reilly discusses an episode which exemplifies the fact that some of us take issue with the idea of religious freedom. Although, none will admit it, and probably don't even realize it.

Bill tells of an incident involving his (then) FNC co-worker, Brit Hume, and goes on to editorialize about it. Specifically, during the unfortunate, and highly publicized, marital distress of professional golfer Tiger Woods, Mr. Hume opined on-air that, being a Buddhist, Mr. Woods' faith doesn't offer the same "forgiveness and redemption" as Christianity.

Mr. Hume then recommended that Tiger convert to the Christian religion, thereby he would not only help himself but be an example to others. After advising this, Hume received some strong criticism and equally strong support. Which side was correct? Let us try to determine.

O'Reilly's assessment of the matter was that Brit Hume was simply giving his opinion, which is what he gets paid for. Furthermore, he said the "Far Left press" was characterizing Hume as a "religious fanatic" for saying what he did. He went on to quote an editorial from his more favored "conservative *Washington Times*," which expressed the opinion that the liberal media displayed a growing "anti-religious bigotry," for criticizing Mr. Hume. (My question is: How, exactly, was the [liberal] media being anti-religious by suggesting that one's religion is their personal decision and Mr. Hume should mind his own business?)

In his three-and-one-half page report on the episode, O'Reilly expressed one other note-worthy opinion, in which he declared to understand how Hume's remarks might seem offensive to Buddhists. With that, Bill at least indicates he gets the fact that announcing one's feelings about their belief as being somehow "better" is wrong. It also illustrates why all his other remarks, defending Hume, as well as those from the *Washington Times*, and Mr. Hume's original declaration itself, are equally wrong. It is because Mr. Hume's advice, and any attempt at defending it, smacks of hubris and intolerance.

Imagine (and I admit, this is going to be a really big stretch of the imagination) that Brit Hume, a professional commentator representing Fox News, were a Muslim. Suppose he had recommended Tiger Woods convert to Islam.

What do you think the response would have been? My guess is Mr. Hume would have been characterized a religious fanatic by not only this country's liberal but conservative establishments and everyone (with the possible exception of Muslims) in between! Had this been what happened, my opinion is that every condemnation would have been deserved. The actual comment, using the word "Christian," was equally entitled to the same. Even if no specific faith had been named, the comment still warranted reprimand because what it effectively said was: *My* religion is better than *your* religion! That attitude is not the American way.

That attitude is also not the Christian way. But many Christians think that way. Some members of all religions do. It's almost like they view religion as a sporting event and feel the need to shout down fans of the other team. Which brings to mind another reason why Brit Hume was wrong in what he said about Buddhism vs. Christianity. For a commentator it was unprofessional because he was *rooting*.

Some of us see the mere existence of other religions as threatening to ours. Religions are not threatening. Religious *fanatics* are threatening. We all view our particular religion as the only true path to salvation. But by what right does that allow for the ridicule of other beliefs? One of the ideas Bill O'Reilly expresses, on page 67 of his book, which I am in complete agreement with, is that he tries to leave the judgment of others to God. (In other words, he minds his own business.)

However, when it comes to religion, a lot of us find it difficult to mind our own business. We all want our beliefs to be respected, but whether out of arrogance, fear, or insecurity about our own beliefs we often fail to respect the beliefs of those who disagree.

I once received one of those misleading, phony-baloney e-mails, which showed the picture of a new, one-dollar coin. It promulgated the notion that the words "In God We Trust" were omitted and we should refuse to accept it as currency. I vetted it and found it to be false. ("In God We Trust" was imprinted on the edge. However, it has since been changed back to the face.) Then I replied to ALL, of course. First, after showing its inaccuracy, I quoted Jesus Christ: "Render unto Caesar the things which are Caesar's, and unto God the things that are God's." Second, I added my own point of view: "If God is in one's heart, one does not need the word 'God' on one's money." Not long after that, I had a conversation about the e-mail with a Christian woman, who is educated as well as intelligent (experience has taught me the two don't always go hand-in-hand). Her exclamation, even after knowing the e-mail to be a lie, was: "Well, I see your point – BUT – no atheists are going to control what I think!" HUH? (By the way, if you pay attention you will notice that, almost invariably, when people say they "see your point" they really don't, and the next words out of their mouths will be "BUT" followed by some sort of *disclaimer*.)

Bill O'Reilly, someone else who is apparently both educated and intelligent, once did an interview with a representative of the American Humanist Association (a.k.a. atheists), whose organization had taken out public ads around Christmas time. The ads read: "Why believe in a god? Just be good for goodness' sake." O'Reilly's position, as I recall, centered on (his judgment) that they should have only used the second sentence, because the question ("Why believe in a god?") was hurtful. Again, HUH? I wasn't hurt!

Furthermore, it can be argued that Humanism is the most selfless, and even courageous, of all beliefs. The late Humanist and renowned author Kurt Vonnegut described Humanism as being decent because it's right, not because we believe we will suffer or be repaid after we die. In other words, "Why believe in a god? Just be good for goodness' sake." I think the interview would have been much more interesting and entertaining, as well as *intelligent*, if O'Reilly had tried to answer the ad's question, rather than question the right to ask it.

There is one last thought I want to include about freedom of religion, it was presented in the book *A History of Knowledge* by Charles Van Doren, who is most remembered for the quiz show scandal of the 1950's. Aside from that, Mr. Van Doren is a scholar, teacher, editor, and author of several books. His explanation as to why our country's Founding Fathers included the concept of religious freedom in the First Amendment to the Constitution is that many of them, especially Thomas Jefferson, were deists. They believed in God but did not adhere to any specific religion. They felt we should be free to worship in whatever manner we chose. Even if some peoples' choice would bring them damnation, government should not force their choice upon them. The people must be allowed to make mistakes, otherwise; how would they "grow up?"

One would be inclined to believe that T.J. and the rest of the Founding Dads also realized that some kids never grow up (without a little help). My mother was not the only influential person in my life who had a penchant for maxims. My dad, as well, would occasionally impart sage advice in easy to remember form. One of his proverbs, which helped me grow up, was simply this: "To be respected – show respect."

Freedom of Speech

Like freedom of religion, freedom of speech is protected by the First Amendment, of the original ten amendments to the U.S. Constitution (a.k.a. The Bill of Rights). Before discussing the right to free speech and how we perceive it in America today, this might be as good a time as any to browse the Bill of Rights itself.

The First Congress created the Bill of Rights to augment and clarify the Constitution. As stated in its Preamble, "... in order to prevent misconstruction or abuse of its powers ...." The most striking aspect, to me, about the amendments in the Bill of Rights is that they are all rather vague. Each of the ten amendments is short and to the point. They each propose one or more idea of law, example (Third Amendment): "No Soldier shall, in time of peace be quartered in any house, without the consent of the Owner, nor in time of war, but in a manner to be prescribed by law." That's all. It is left up to the reader to determine what manner the law should prescribe. One would think the vagueness might promote rather than prevent "misconstruction." Probably, on occasion, one might be correct.

However, remember Professor Van Doren's insight into the wisdom of the men who wrote The Constitution and "The Bill": The people must be allowed to make mistakes, otherwise; how would they "grow up?" So grow up we did, guided by the Founding Fathers' advice, which they worded to be open to interpretation. Thus allowing us to decide, not what their words meant, but how we should apply them as we grew and, more importantly, *changed*. They were truly men of remarkable genius!

The amendments that make up the Bill of Rights, and all subsequent Constitutional amendments (there are currently twenty-seven in total, the last one being ratified in 1992), are still often discussed and debated. As the Founding Fathers knew they would be.

But the first two amendments probably receive the most attention and scrutiny, as well as cause the most debate.

Amendment One: "Congress shall make no law respecting an establishment of religion, or prohibiting the free exercise thereof; or abridging the freedom of speech, or of the press; or the right of the people peaceably to assemble, and to petition the Government for a redress of grievances."

Amendment Two: "A well regulated Militia, being necessary to the security of a free State, the right of the people to keep and bear Arms, shall not be infringed." (We will have a conversation about this one, at length, later on.)

Now, let us return to our discussion about freedom of speech.

William J. Brennan Jr., United States Supreme Court Justice, appointed by Republican President Dwight D. Eisenhower, declared that a "bedrock principle" of the First Amendment, was that the state cannot outlaw a citizen's promotion of an idea because other citizens are offended or don't agree. Noam Chomsky, Institute Professor (the highest honor they bestow) at M.I.T. and self proclaimed socialist, said to embrace free speech you must embrace the free speech of ideas you don't like.

Two opinions, from two learned and accomplished men, from opposite ends of the political scale, which assert the same value: When it comes to free speech – if you don't like it – TOUGH COOKIES!

Sometimes I find that as hard to swallow as anyone else. My skin crawls when I see the American flag burned. But the Supreme Court declared it permissible under the First Amendment. My blood boils when I see members of a so-called "church," which I shall not name because all they really want is publicity, protesting at a funeral, about something the deceased had nothing to do with. But the Supremes said they're good to go. I am stunned by the open display of a swastika. But the Sups said live with it, so I do.

However, when given calm consideration, it is obvious the Supreme Court is right. It is the only course that makes fair sense. If I want the freedom to march on Wall Street, with the AFL-CIO, and call investment bankers "Robber Barons" (which I have done), I must be willing to not only hear their response, but also defend their right to say it. THAT is where the beauty be found!

If plutocrats, demagogues, hypocrites, or subversives are gagged they will simply spread their lies and hatred to gullible, unsuspecting victims under-the-radar. It is only freedom of speech that allows and, most indispensably, *entices* them to spout publicly. When they do they expose themselves to *the mirror of truth.* Their own words give us the arms we need to shoot down their fraud.

The right to free speech is the weapon of freedom loving people. The abuse of it, by those who would steal that freedom, is our ammunition.

Guns

The Second Amendment, *the idea:* The Right to Bear Arms. *The question:* Can we protect that right, for freedom loving Americans, and keep guns away from those who would do evil? *The answer:* It can be done. It is, in many other countries. *The problem:* Many freedom and *gun* loving Americans don't like the how. *The how:* REGULATION.

The gun control debate generally follows these lines: Supporters of gun control want the availability of guns to be regulated in such a way that will keep, or at least virtually keep, guns out of the hands of dangerous people. They contend that the fewer guns there are around, the less violent crimes will be committed. Gun advocates oppose just about any proposal to regulate guns in any way. Their stance is that the Second Amendment gives them the right to own guns – PERIOD – and any regulation will lead to more regulation, making it more difficult to own guns. Furthermore, the gun lovers say, the more guns there are around, the less violent crimes will be committed.

This issue seems to be a prime candidate for the "Judge Judy Test." Which side's arguments make the most sense?

Both sides give examples and statistics that demonstrate the correctness of their arguments. Simultaneously, both sides claim the examples and statistics of the other side are skewed and misleading. So let us then dispense with the examples and statistics, and simply look at both arguments from the standpoint of logic.

The Supreme Court has ruled to uphold the Second Amendment multiple times. Regardless of the fact that a civilian Militia is no longer necessary, the right of private citizens to own guns is a done-deal. Therefore, the only question is: Should that right be regulated?

Pretty much any one of us who is old enough to read can name several tragic incidents involving guns that were obtained legally. To keep things simple, let's examine just one. Would a law prohibiting the sale of a firearm to a person deemed mentally unstable have saved the lives of six people and the brain damage to Congresswoman Gabrielle Giffords in Arizona, all shot by someone who was mentally unstable? One would think so. But gun advocates believe if everyone at the scene had a gun the incident could have been prevented. Logic dictates that assumption leaves too much to chance.

Would you be comfortable knowing that everyone around you was able to pull a gun out of their coat, and hopefully was a good shot? [O]r would you feel more secure in the knowledge that the chance of someone having a gun was very slim, and if someone did, they were stable and proficient with it?

If it is true that more guns mean less crime, should we arm all of our Kindergarteners because of the rash of tragic school shootings? If that idea sounds stupid, it's because it is. But it reflects the logic of gun advocates. Doesn't it?

The argument by gun proponents, claiming that any regulation will lead to more regulation and make it more difficult to own a gun, is quite frankly a crybaby contention. I admit that I agree with them 100%. But TOUGH COOKIES! Anything that has the potential of harming someone else *should* be strictly regulated.

I smoke cigars, and I must pay high "sin" taxes when I buy them, as well as abide by strict regulations regarding where I can light up. I am, therefore, uncomfortable with the idea that, in case I forget where I am and inadvertently ignite one, I might get my brains blown out for it!

Exactly who are the gun advocates? The leading group in this country is the National Rifle Association (NRA). Ostensibly operating as non-profit defenders of the Second Amendment, the NRA lobbies politicians to enact laws that make it as easy as possible for anyone to buy a gun. The NRA's biggest contributors are gun manufacturers. Do you think that might have some influence on their philosophical position?

Following the Gabrielle Giffords incident, the NRA was invited by President Obama to discuss gun control. Their CEO said the Administration wanted to repeal the Second Amendment, so why should he meet with them? Well, one reason which comes to mind would be to try to defend your side. But, of course, if you realize going in that your side is indefensible then indeed why should you meet with them?

Gun lovers have a couple of favored slogans. One is: "Guns don't kill people – people kill people!" Once again, I agree with them 100%. And with their own words they demonstrate how illogical their arguments are. Since "people kill people," any sane person would support keeping guns away from dangerous people. Am I suggesting that all gun lovers are insane? Not at all. (Although it has been repeatedly proven that some are. Has it not?) They're just biased in their thinking. Biased, either from that sense of "entitlement" we get from The Constitution, which makes a lot of us feel deserving but should not have to pay for anything. [O]r biased from pure, selfish greed, like that of the NRA and the gun makers, who gladly put profit ahead of their fellow Americans' safety.

The other favored slogan of gunnies is: "If guns are outlawed – only outlaws will have guns!" This is certainly a justifiable concern. However, like the Founding Fathers, to advance and improve our society we must be creative. A solution worth exploring, which might eliminate that problem as well as other criminal activity such as illegal drug trafficking, or at least greatly reduce them, is proposed in the book *How the U.S Won the War on Drugs* by H. Owen Stevens: Get rid of cash. If we became a totally cashless society who could rob a bank? If we regulate (not "outlaw") guns, how would dangerous people get them in a cashless society? The black market doesn't take credit cards!

The NRA was originally an advocacy group for gun owners. Its primary function was to teach the safe handling of guns, which it still does. But now the NRA's primary function is as an advocacy group for gun makers. They lobby and contribute to politicians to keep gun laws as relaxed as possible. They also promote the myth that more guns will mean less gun violence.

In poll after poll, gun owners, including "a majority" of NRA members say they favor stricter gun laws, such as background checks, to keep guns out of the hands of dangerous people. Why do these same people then vote siding with the NRA and against their own safety? PROPAGANDA! The NRA and the demagogue politicians and pundits in its employ have gun owners convinced their "enemies" want to repeal the Second Amendment and *take their guns away!*

While campaigning for the Presidency, Donald Trump latched-on to the NRA. He understands how propaganda works and how powerful the NRA's line is. After the Orlando, Florida nightclub shootings, Trump told a crowd how he'd wished some "good guy" with a gun would have been there. Of course, he got cheers and applause because he addressed the crowd's anger, which is an emotion ... and THAT, is PROPAGANDA.

Finally, let me throw one more thing out there for your consideration. The NRA and Donald Trump say more guns will mean less gun violence. All studies show that Black Americans are killed by guns "two times" more often than Whites. So why don't the NRA and Donald Trump advocate for all Black Americans to own guns? I have a couple of ideas why. What do you think?

My conclusions are: No responsible gun owner should, nor (I think) will, have their gun(s) taken away. Anyone who wants a gun – or for that matter – a bazooka, a tank, or a jet fighter – ought to be able to have it. AS-LONG-AS-THEY can prove they are not dangerous, go through initial as well as recurrent training, and pay substantial testing, licensing and registration fees to fund their Second Amendment "entitlement."

And *finally*, finally – a footnote: Long after I finished writing the above essay, another mass gun killing occurred. On October 1, 2017 over 500 people were injured and nearly 60 were killed, in Las Vegas, Nevada. This latest incident (for now) made me think that maybe we have been approaching the U.S. gun problem in the wrong way all along. I wrote an article addressing it. (It can be found at the end of this book, in Appendix A.)

My ideas, in the article and in the above essay, might or might not work. Your ideas might or might not work. My only hope is that everyone's ideas get discussed and given consideration, with open minds, so everyone might start *thinking about what we're thinking.*

Healthcare

Although The Declaration of Independence refers to "Life, Liberty and the pursuit of Happiness," this being derived from John Locke's 1689 assertion of the rights to "Life, *Health,* Liberty or Possessions" (emphasis added), the right to health care is not specifically addressed in The Constitution of The United States of America, the supreme law of the land. Nevertheless, although health care is not guaranteed legally, many feel strongly that it is morally. Others feel, even this is not so. Therefore, in the 21st century, America is still the only major nation in the world that does not have some type of Universal Health Care. The debate rages on. One major political party refuses to consider Universal Health Care because they are in the health insurance companies' pockets. The other major political party can only do so much ... because they are in the health insurance companies' pockets!

In my research of information for this discussion, I came across two speeches, one pro and one con. They were given by educated men, who are passionate about their respective view. Therefore, I will let their views make the arguments for and against our right to health care. I will also interject my own conclusions. And I encourage you to thoughtfully do likewise. Please keep in mind, whether it's called "Socialized Medicine" or "Obama-Care," which are both propaganda terms, we will be talking about the concept of *Universal* Healthcare.

The first speech I will reference, the pro, was given by the Independent Senator from Vermont, Bernard Sanders, in 2009. (If you would like to read the entire speech it is on *huffingtonpost.com*. Just *Google:* "Is Healthcare a right" to find it listed.) First he cited some statistics, such as, the United States spends nearly two times as much per person on health care than any other nation, but we are graded number "37" in "health system performance" by the World Health Organization. Also, GM was spending more per car produced to fund health care for their workers than for the steel needed to produce it.

He went on to state that most Americans favor affordable health care for all. Therefore, according to Sen. Sanders, the only question is: How do we achieve it?

He promotes Medicare for all, with a publicly funded single-payer system. That is effectively an insurance pool, from which all health care costs are paid. As evidence of its benefit he pointed to our current Medicare setup, in addition to Medicaid and the VA program. These are far less costly to operate than private health insurance, because private health insurers are corporations with the primary function of maximizing profit. Additionally, private health insurance corporations incur the costs of advertising, political campaign contributions and lobbying, which further increase our cost for their product.

Senator Sanders related that the U.S.A.'s largest health insurance corporations had a consolidated profit increase of one-hundred-and-seventy percent from 2003 to 2007. As nearly 10% of Americans were standing on the Unemployment line, with no health insurance, CEO compensation at the top seven health insurance companies averaged $14.2 million.

Senator Bernard Sanders is no Pollyanna. He conceded that affordable Universal Healthcare will be a difficult goal to achieve. The private interests, making embarrassing profits from Americans' pain, won't go down without a fight. They will pour as much money as they feel they must into the pockets of politicians, so they can keep taking advantage of the current system. As confirmation, I recount the fact that by the time so-called "Obama-Care" was signed into law, the private health insurance industry had called in their markers. They demanded, and received, a final bill that was a shell of the major overhaul it was intended to have been. The most important victory, for them, was the complete removal of its backbone, the much anticipated "Public Option." And the fight is still not over.

However, in the conclusion to his speech, Sen. Sanders reminded us that there is always hope. Referencing the struggles for civil rights and women's rights, he summed up by saying justice in America might get delayed – but not denied. "We shall overcome!"

The Patient Protection and Affordable Care Act, was signed into law on March 23, 2010. It was amended and replaced, seven days later, by the Healthcare and Education Reconciliation Act, which is the proper name for "Obama-Care."

The proposed Healthcare Reform Bill became a Health and Education Bill. And unceasingly since it was passed, although they agreed to it, Republicans have vowed to get it repealed. Whenever Republican Presidential candidates announce their intentions to do so they are cheered and applauded. I am absolutely stupefied by this!

Remember that most Americans support some form of affordable health care *for all*. One of Donald Trump's campaign platforms was "repeal and replace Obama-Care," and it helped get him elected. Trump, of course, never had a clue how to do it – and when people began to see what the rest of his party had in mind, they thought "Obama-Care" ain't that bad!

Now on to the second speech, the con.

An argument that Healthcare is not a right was given by, one, Leonard Peikoff, Ph. D., in 1993 against President Clinton's similar Healthcare proposal. (Again, if you want to read it entirely, *Google:* "Is Healthcare a right" to find it listed. It is on *bdt.com*.)

Peikoff opined that Universal Healthcare is socialized medicine, which he expounds to be akin to all socialism as not practical or moral. He explained that his theory is based on *his interpretation* of the Declaration of Independence, i.e., "Life, Liberty and the pursuit of Happiness" does not guarantee those things but only guarantees the opportunity to work for them. My "favorite" idea from his speech is perhaps that work is our right – turning others into slaves is not.

He contended that Universal Healthcare would destroy the medical profession, by forcing doctors to hand out medical care for free. And he went on to claim that the middle class is hurt most by these types of programs, because they pay the bulk of the taxes to fund them. (At this point in the discussion, as an "average" American, I will say that I agree we pay the bulk of taxes. But I assert that using taxes to fund social programs fairly helps rather than hurts us.) He wondered: Could individuals afford health care themselves? And he answered himself by citing our taxes, which he considers government seizure of the peoples' money, to be confirmation that we can.

Are you beginning to see, as I did, the contradictions in Peikoff's theory? He claims that Universal Healthcare is a handout. But he says that our taxes pay for it. Read on, it gets even better!

After asserting that our taxes prove we can afford health care on our own, he allows that some cannot. His solution to their plight? Charity. My questions: If instead of paying taxes to fund some form of Universal Healthcare, we are forced to shop the private insurers and donate to a charity that will cover the indigent, which system do you think would be more expensive? Which do you think would be fairer? Which do you think would be easier to guarantee? Furthermore, on the subject of taxes, Peikoff believes they too, like charity, ought to be voluntary. (This was not addressed directly in his Healthcare speech, I learned it by researching his background.)

Those who agree with Peikoff's views espouse the free market (Laissez-faire) philosophy. They feel that if left alone, society will necessarily do the right thing. That the affordability of health care, or any other "product," will take care of itself, and altruism will take care of the rest. (Here comes another contradiction.) They simultaneously view altruism as "destructive." (I plan to deal with Peikoff and his cohorts in a later chapter. They are followers of Ayn Rand. Look up her views on the "destructiveness" of altruism and the "virtue" of selfishness.)

Senator Bernard Sanders' philosophy, as I interpret it, contends that we must protect ourselves from *ourselves.* He considers health care a basic need, equal to the needs for education, police, and fire protection.

Do you sincerely believe that big health insurance corporations, if left alone, will necessarily do the right thing or do you think they will necessarily put profits first? Given the nature of human nature, do you think that if taxes were made voluntary, like charity, everyone would willingly pay their fair share?

If Sen. Sanders' Universal Healthcare Plan were adopted as he describes it we will not have Socialized Medicine and doctors would not hand out services free of charge. We would fund a pool to pay medical care providers, which is exactly what private insurers do. And health care could still be administered by private companies – BUT – with regulations to protect us from price gouging, unfairly high premiums, or refusal of services because we are "sick."

The con, declared by Peikoff, is frankly a *con*. Those who work for the things they desire might not always have the ability to. And when they don't, a Universal Health Insurance Pool would *prevent* their needing to be given health care free of charge. It would also prevent private health insurance plutocrats from getting rich off other people's distress.

Illegal Immigration

A few years ago, I watched a BBC documentary about the United States. One episode was all about Texas. (Coincidently, I watched it while living in Kansas City, Missouri, just before moving to where I live now – Texas.) In it, the estimation was made that if all the illegal, Mexican aliens could be sent back across the border immediately at least half the hotels and restaurants in Texas would go out of business. This illuminates the twofold character of the Immigration Control problem: (1) Illegitimate workers taking legitimate jobs. (2) Greed.

A 2006 *USA TODAY* article, entitled "Immigrants Claim Pivotal Role in Economy," written by reporters David J. Lynch and Chris Woodyard, discussed how illegal workers are essential to some American businesses. Examples: Restaurants, hotels, construction and farming. The article cited that uneducated and unskilled immigrant workers diminish wages for similarly qualified American workers. But they also help keep product prices down and business owners' profits up.

Remember President George W. Bush's "Guest Worker Program" proposal? He promoted it by claiming that illegal workers are here doing jobs Americans don't want to. Really? The *USA TODAY* article reported that the Census Bureau found 2.3 million jobless Americans were last employed in businesses currently employing 7.9 million foreign workers.

The above *USA TODAY* article also referenced the coexisting problem of emigration, not of American citizens, but of our jobs. That is, sometimes the option is not American vs. foreign worker but American work being sent to a foreign country. Remember what Pat Buchanan said? Global American companies now want, expect and get tremendous tax incentives, government subsidies, authorization to bring foreign workers here because they can pay them less, free-rein to send their manufacturing plants and jobs outside U.S. borders and the freedom to import their own products back here without tariffs to be sold to American citizens, as credit for their contributions to our elected representatives. As I indicated, a dual dilemma: (1) Illegitimate workers taking legitimate jobs. (2) Greed.

Even more unfortunately, there is another, rather sickening aspect to the immigration control problem – slavery. According to the website of the Federal Bureau of Investigation, *fbi.gov*, the smuggling, buying and selling of human beings exists today – in the United States of America. Forced to work at tough, manual labor jobs or as prostitutes, people get small pay or none at all, and are routinely starved and beaten.

With the lucrative nature of illegal immigration, it's no wonder that it is challenging to control. For illegal aliens it affords the chance to live, and work at legitimate jobs, in the USA. For dishonest employers, it's an opportunity to take advantage of them at half the pay, or none at all if they utilize the slave trade.

In 1986, Congress approved the Immigration Reform and Control Act, which shifted emphasis from border patrol to employer accountability. Under it, if employers could not document the legality of their workers, they faced fines and sanctions. Congress thought it was a good idea, and it sounds like it still would be. But guess who it helped? The crooked employers. They simply circumvented the law by using "subcontractors" to supply illegal workers. By doing so, they avoided liability because, technically, "their workers" were not "their employees." As a bonus they got to pay the poor souls even less, because the subcontractor got part of their wages. (Incidentally, right now, unscrupulous employers are using this hiring strategy against naturally born, American citizens, too. It allows them the ability to avoid providing benefits. And to, of course, pay lower wages as well.) By the 1990s focus was shifted back to Border Patrol, since the "employer sanctions" program was deemed inefficient. (Speaking of inefficiency, after "9/11," Border Patrol was folded into the newly created Department of Homeland Security. Since then I have wondered, as has Pat Buchanan in

Where the Right Went Wrong: Why do we need a Department of Homeland Security – supposedly to defend the homeland – when we already have a Department of Defense?)

In fact, since the 1980s illegal immigration has "increased dramatically" and, since the mid 1990s, has "surpassed the number of legal immigrants," according to the Pew Hispanic Center.

It's quite a complicated mess, isn't it? And since every attempted remedy only seems to make matters worse, it is monumentally frustrating as well. So what's the solution? Obviously, giving up is not it. And discussing it, as we are, isn't either. However, discussing it to find creative solutions, without giving up, might be? But, as with anything else, only if we demand our representatives listen and act.

If slippery employers utilize mercenary "subcontractors," shouldn't we demand laws be re-written to attack the subcontractors?

If businesses are sending American jobs overseas, exacerbating the unemployment problem, don't we need to demand the laws (that allow it) be repealed?

If we want new jobs created (to replace the ones that will never come back) how about Border Guards?

As with Universal Healthcare, it would be Pollyannaish to think illegal immigration will be easy to fix. Why? Greed. If you and I can come up with viable solutions, just by paying a little attention, don't you think our representatives can, too? Certainly, but their agenda is not ours. However, the fault is ours. We vote for them.

This brings us to Donald Trump's wall. He got himself elected, partly, by promising to build a wall along the Mexican border and "guaranteeing" that Mexico would pay for it. Of course, Mexico said NO. So after taking office, he said we would "finance" it but Mexico will pay us back. They still say NO.

Trump said: Walls work – ask Israel. Being unable to literally ask Israel, I looked it up. Israel has a 400 mile wall along the Palestinian border. The U.S./Mexican border is over 2,000 miles. Additionally, Israel has other layers of protection, like *troops,* not just a wall. Israel, along with every other nation on Earth, still suffers terrorist attacks. In fact, thanks to Israel's wall, in 2016 they had 58 terrorist attacks. The U.S.A. had 38. (University of Maryland, Global Terrorism Database) Walls work? Go ahead, ask Israel. Ask France. The Maginot Line was a fortress the French built to hold back the Germans in WWI and again in WWII. It worked, too. The only problem was the German Army just marched to the end of the French border and walked around it. Ask Russia. The Berlin Wall was a piece of "Swiss cheese" for its entire existence and was eventually toppled by *the people.* Even "The Great Wall of China" (I've visited it. Big wall!) was not just a wall. It had (has) fortresses and outposts that were manned by troops. Still, China was conquered twice in its history. And while he's at it, why doesn't Trump want to build a wall along the Canadian border? There are illegal entries from Canada as well as Mexico. Maybe Trump doesn't think (that voters think) Canadians are criminals, drug dealers, rapists, murderers, and of course, some of them are nice people. So, to keep his believers believing in him, Trump cracked down on documented, legal aliens who (Oops!) forgot to get their visas renewed. And, of course, because they're easy to catch. Meanwhile, illegal foreigners are being smuggled across our borders by the tractor-trailer-load!

The reason our representatives don't listen to us is because we don't listen to them. Many of us simply seek to hear what we want to hear. Consequently, we don't elect representatives we elect politicians with their own agendas. As long as we do, we'll continue to be "represented" by those who are obligated to self-interested businesses, which gladly pay to lobby them, so they will in turn keep the immigration laws as they are.

<u>Media</u>

From our increasing reliance on electronic media, mainly television, many of our conclusions are conceived instantly, with little or no thought. As Bill O'Reilly suggested (on page 81 of *Pinheads and Patriots):* The American people seem to be losing the ability to scrutinize, which makes us more vulnerable to manipulation by charismatic, phony politicians that only want to gain power. (OH, HOW RIGHT HE WAS!) We are (losing) and they are (gaining).

This phenomenon is not the fault of media. The fault is in our failure to understand the nature of media, specifically electronic media and especially television. Moreover, it is imperative we understand how the nature of the medium is used to influence and even control not only the gullible but also those simply unaware.

Our friend, Professor Charles Van Doren, in *A History of Knowledge,* discussed perhaps the most famous researcher of media ever known. Today he is all but forgotten, but in 1964 he wrote *Understanding Media: The Extensions of Man,* one of the most highly regarded books about media ever published. His name was Marshall McLuhan.

In 1964, before anyone owned a PC or smart-phone, McLuhan's main focus was TV. And due to its nature, TV remains the most influential type of media there is. Despite the fact that computers are virtually instant in providing information they do require some work from the user. TV, on the other hand, is literally instant.

We must search for information on computers, which is sort of like, although certainly much easier than, going to the library. Computers give us what *we* want. TV programmers give us what *they* want. The nature of our relationship with a computer is active. With a TV screen it's passive, we just sit there and soak up information, even if (maybe especially if [?]) we desire not to think. That is why TV is the preferred way to disseminate propaganda, whether that propaganda is positive or negative.

Radio, mostly because it can be "everywhere," is also a powerful tool. But TV holds the advantage over radio due to the addition of visual imagery. Media studies have shown the use of visual images, to reinforce spoken or written information, makes the message easier to retain. (The adage "one picture is worth a thousand words," or some variation of it, is an idea we are all familiar with. Expression of this concept has been attributed to advertising manager Fred Barnard in the 1920s as well as other communicators throughout history, including Napoleon Bonaparte.) This is what gives TV its mighty *one-two*, propaganda *punch!*

Marshall McLuhan is chiefly remembered for his famous aphorism: "The medium is the message." Van Doren remarked that had McLuhan been a scientist (he was an English professor) he would not have made that statement because it's an exaggeration. However, Van Doren defended McLuhan by clarifying that although the medium isn't the entire message, which is what makes it an exaggeration, the medium is some part of the message and always affects the message. A specific example he gave, vital to the understanding of our relationship with today's media, was how McLuhan explained that with electronic media, information moves so fast we don't get a moment to digest it, consideration becomes the identification of patterns. Therefore, conclusions are based on intuition instead of thought.

Conclusions are based on *intuition* instead of *thought*. Remember, all propaganda appeals to our *emotions*, as opposed to our *intellect*.

To disregard the method in which we are presented a message, and only focus on content, is naive. Nevertheless, content is still the primary component. However, when coupled with the "right" method, the message of the content is reinforced in our minds. And the goal of the message is always the same. That being, to motivate us to *act*.

So how can we defend ourselves against messages that would motivate us to act against our own best interests? Van Doren advised that comprehending the nature of the medium is not enough, knowledge and understanding of the environment it attempts to create in our minds is the key. To put it another, even simpler way, in the words of Dr. Mark Goulston: "Think about what you're thinking." I realize I have been pounding out this idea repeatedly. It is why I decided to write this book. But I will now reveal a caveat: It's not always easy! The reason is something referred to as "backfire." And expert propagandists, who understand backfire, routinely convince not only the gullible, but also those simply unaware, to act against their own best interests.

The Phenomenon of Backfire:

On July 11, 2010, the *Boston Globe* carried an article entitled "How Facts Backfire," by Joe Keohane. In it, Keohane did an in-depth examination of the phenomenon. Most of what follows is based on what he found.

The term backfire was coined during a series of studies done at the University of Michigan from 2005 – 2006. The researchers discovered that when people have preconceived notions, i.e., beliefs, which are incorrect, and are presented with the opposing correct facts, they rarely change their minds. Contrarily, more often than not, they become even more convinced that their original beliefs are true. This curiosity is what the scientists at U of M named backfire. Brendan Nyhan, the lead researcher, explained it as "a natural defense mechanism" because "it's absolutely threatening to admit you're wrong."

(It is worth noting here that although the U of M study provides scientific evidence as well as a convenient, one word description for the phenomenon, backfire, the awareness of it is not new. The concept, as a trait of human nature, has been evident to those in the business of persuasion for ages. Dr. Nyhan's explanation of the idea was echoed by Mark Twain, perhaps this nation's greatest communicator and social observer, who put it this way: "A man cannot be comfortable without his own approval.")

Backfire, is a form of what is known as "motivated reasoning." And the more strongly we feel about an issue the more motivated we are to hold on to it and the harder it is to change our minds. Additionally, the more insecure or threatened we feel the less likely we are to listen to dissenting opinions. Keohane pointed out how this clarifies why demagogues keep people disturbed. The more fearful people are – the easier they are to manipulate. (They're gonna take your guns away! Etc.)

In his *Boston Globe* article, Mr. Keohane described how chillingly harmful backfire can be. He expressed how we prefer to think our conclusions are based on reasoned thought. But in fact, we regularly base our conclusions on our beliefs. Thereby, we pick and choose the facts that coincide with our preconceptions. This is so terribly destructive because it leads us to the automatic acceptance of wrong data, simply because it supports what we (already) believe. Support assures us we are correct and *closes our minds* to the consideration of new data, which might be right. THEN – we go to the voting booth. (Get ready – here it comes again: Think about what you're thinking!)

For us consumers of information, trying to keep acutely aware of content and method and how our brains interpret both can be exhausting. That is why our brains rely on innate shortcuts like intuition. And that is why we can be easy suckers for demagogic manipulation. Joe Keohane wrapped up his article by discussing the possible solution, proposed by Professor Nyhan. He [Nyhan] suggested that those who report our information hold their sources accountable, and publicly admonish them for spreading misinformation. (For a great example, see pages 11-15 of *Pinheads and Patriots* by Bill O'Reilly.) Keohane remarked though, the solution had a downside. Specifically, demagogues, propagandists, and phony politicians are not easily shamed. (For a great example, see pages 11-15 of *Pinheads and Patriots* by Bill O'Reilly.)

Therefore, if we can't rely on our media professionals to clear the clutter for us, or on pundits to admit when they are wrong, and if thinking about what we are thinking can be so exhausting, what can *we* do to protect *ourselves*?

Simplify the process! When we think about any information, just break it down to the basic question of: "Does it make sense?" It works for Judge Judy, and it has worked for me, too. Asking if something makes sense, and following a simple chain of logic, gets us to the more important understanding of: Does it make sense *for us*? Put another way: Is it in *our* best interest or that of the entity selling it?

Following a chain of logic, this now brings us to an examination of specific medium, the messenger. Since the medium is some part of – and always affects – the message, understanding *their* interest beforehand wins half the battle. All we need to consider then is whether or not the message is in *our* interest as well.

Television broadcasters, our main focus, have two predominant business models; public and corporate. The mission of Public Broadcasting as stated on its website, *pbs.org*, is to provide programming that will educate, inform and inspire. The mission of corporate broadcasters is to generate profit. Therefore, which model would you think creates a built-in agenda?

We have previously discussed Bill O'Reilly's opinion that PBS leans Left, and the White house once said FNC was "a wing of the Republican Party." Both accusations are, most likely, extreme. However, it would be safe to say each entity has its own slant, if deliberate or not. All entities do, including you and me. But whether one is a Liberal watching PBS, or a Conservative viewing FNC, it is not in our best interest to do so uncritically. In order to avoid the phenomenon of backfire, the "does it make sense [?]" approach is our only defense.

Personally, I tend to keep my guard up a little higher when watching a corporate, broadcast network. That is because their goal of making a profit necessarily builds-in the agenda of selling me something. Naturally, this is done through advertising. The only way they can gauge their success is with ratings, which measure the size of their audience. The higher the ratings, the more advertisers they attract, and the more they can charge said advertisers. Therefore, it is in their best interest to reinforce the beliefs of their audience, which is not always in the best interest of the audience.

In 2011, Glenn Beck did his final broadcast on FNC. Leading up to it, he intimated that he would be moving on to more important things. The truth is his ratings were plummeting. By going too far, in not only reinforcing but pandering to his audiences' beliefs he drove people and, more importantly, advertisers away. (See: "It's Official: *Glenn Beck* Ratings Down 30% From 2010," *mediamatters.org*, March 30, 2011)

The demise of the *Glenn Beck* program should encourage all open-minded, clear thinking people tremendously. It validates Abraham Lincoln: "... you cannot fool all the people all the time." It validates Bill O'Reilly: the patriots outnumber the pinheads. And it confirms the wisdom of Dr. Mark Goulston: "Think about what you're thinking," as well as Judge Judy: "Does it make sense?"

Granted, Beck's TV show was an extreme example of insulting demagoguery. But now that enough Americans have demonstrated the ability to realize it did not make sense, and get it removed from history's greatest propaganda tool, there is hope that more of us are starting to think about what we're thinking.

Politicians

In this discussion, I want to focus on politicians rather than politics in general, because politics is simply a process used to get things done. As a process, politics is not dangerous. Politicians, who would misuse and abuse the process, are dangerous (somewhat like the difference between religion and religious fanatics).

I am reminded of another one of my father's truisms. Whenever I would say, upon hearing some disturbing news, something like "we live in a cruel (or evil) world" my father always corrected me by remarking: "The world is not evil – people are evil."

That is not meant to insinuate all politicians are evil. But most of us can think of certain ones who we feel are, or are at least unprincipled. Here's another gem to mull over, it was expressed by Abraham Lincoln: "If you want to test a man's character, give him power." Power comes in many forms. In today's societies, especially in ours, money equals power.

While I served as a local, union vice-president, I attended some of the annual stockholders' meetings of the company I worked for. Occasionally, shareholder advocate, Evelyn Y. Davis, who is both famous and feared in the world of "Big Business," would be in attendance. I once heard her remark that politicians are only interested in two things – "votes and contributions."

Bill O'Reilly commented in *Pinheads and Patriots* (page 143) about the origins of "lobbying" and how the term came about. (It has to do with President U.S. Grant supposedly holding-court every morning in a hotel's lobby. It's a quaint story that I had heard before, but unfortunately it isn't true. I looked it up. [Obviously, Bill didn't. See what I mean about accepting "facts"?] Actually, lobbying dates back to history's earliest governments, such as Greece and Rome.) Lobbying is protected, as a practice, under the First Amendment: "... to petition the Government for a redress of grievances." The option to petition by giving gifts, donations, and campaign contributions is not specified. In certain countries these are considered bribes and are criminal. However, in the United States they are all legal.

President Barak Obama was known to be the greatest fundraiser ever to run for office. And if money equals power – power equals votes – and that was chiefly why he became The Chief. Unfortunately, many of his contributors, the ones with the biggest stakes in the game, hedged their bets by donating to his opposition as well. The danger of this system is evident in the stalemate we still see in Washington.

This is a good time to take a closer look at the two individuals I earlier promised to, President Obama and GE CEO Jeffrey Immelt.

About President Obama, I have said that I believe he agrees with fair income redistribution but he was hindered by his obligations. That brings us to Mr. Immelt, who exemplifies the conundrum. Immelt was appointed by Obama to head his "Economic Recovery Advisory Board." President Obama is, of course, a Democrat. Mr. Immelt, however, is a Republican. GE, the company he runs,* contributes pretty much equally to both major parties and was a "major contributor" to Barak Obama's 2008 campaign, according to website *OpenSecrets.org*. (*Note: In 2017, Jeffrey Immelt announced he would be stepping down from GE CEO.)

Stated in a *New York Times* article of March 24, 2011, GE made $14.2 billion in 2010 and paid "no" tax. *Times* reporter David Kocieniewski wrote that over the past decade the company spent more than $200 million on lobbying. And GE's efforts were instrumental in the passage, by President G.W. Bush in 2004, of the (cleverly, flag-waving propaganda, named) "American Jobs Creation Act." This act "created" over $13 billion in annual corporate tax breaks, the bulk favoring GE. While GOP parrots incessantly repeat the tune that corporate tax breaks create jobs the article points out that since 2002 GE has increased its overseas employment, and eliminated "twenty percent" of its American workers.

Why would President Obama appoint the guy who oversaw all this, as the CEO of GE, to be the head of a Board to recover the economy? Did the President truly believe that Mr. Immelt was the best candidate to create American jobs? [O]r might it just be possible that Mr. Obama was fulfilling an obligation?

To President Obama's credit, on his first day in office he issued regulations* on what roles former lobbyists can take in government, and restrictions* on former government officials becoming lobbyists. (*Note: The record indicates that these *regulations* and *restrictions* turned out to be more like *suggestions*.)

Until substantial laws, with "teeth," are passed to restrict gifts, donations, and campaign contributions from lobbyists the deck will remain stacked in favor of the big guns. Until *we the people* make the effort to seek out Independent representatives, not obligated to special interests, we will continue to be the last to eat.

That brings us, again, to President Donald Trump. Capitalizing on his celebrity, Trump portrayed himself as protector of the people against the greedy "big guns" and "special interests." Actually, as principal owner of The Trump Organization, a multi-national conglomerate, Mr. Trump is a *big gun* and a *special interest.*

Nevertheless, Donald Trump convinced enough voters that his wealth was an asset to them because it meant he couldn't be bought. For that reason, although he is a Republican, he is viewed as "independent." FOR THAT REASON (looking on the bright side) Trump's election in 2016 shows that an outsider can now be successful. Further evidence was the election of a third-party candidate as President of France in 2017, the first time that has ever happened in a major world power. We the people are ready for real change!

To play it safe, Trump ran as a Republican because no one has ever been elected President of the United States from a third-party. He also chose the Republican Party, specifically, because he is a master in the art of persuasion and the Republican base is easier to persuade. (We will examine why that is as we move on.) But Trump in 2016, and France in 2017, demonstrates that the world, and America, is ready to elect representatives who are truly INDEPENDENT.

It won't be easy to change the current system, since politicians crave power and that equals money. But as Independent Senator Bernard Sanders (who just might have beaten Trump had he run as an Independent rather than a Democrat) reminded us, justice in America might get delayed – but not denied. "We shall overcome!" Remember too, there are far more patriots than pinheads and plutocrats.

Social Media

Whoever came up with the idea of e-mail deserves to win some kind of award! Actually, it was a man named Ray Tomlinson, and he's won several. E-mail, along with personal websites and social networking, has truly revolutionized communication. Never before has mankind been able to promote our individual agendas with such ease, speed, and volume. The problem (you knew there was a problem) is that so much of it is insulting, self-centered, unmitigated bunk.

Not that many years ago, e-mail was the preferred method of disseminating bunk. Remember those e-mails that flooded your inbox, subtly threatening you with phrases such as: If you don't forward (i.e., agree with) this you are unpatriotic or godless? Remember the ones that were outright racist? How many did you get that were simply lies? How many did you take the time to actually check the veracity of?

Nowadays, e-mail has taken a back-seat to the likes of *Facebook, Twitter* and *YouTube* as well as personal websites and blogs, which are all faster and more effective ways of spreading bunk.

Truth or Fiction and *Snopes* are two websites I use regularly, to check whether an e-mail or *Facebook* post is factual or phony. But I still see so many that are outright fantasy, it is apparent that a great number of people do not bother to check. This is what worries me. This indicates that a great number of people are gullible.

I regularly see *Facebook* posts referring to short videos or to articles that are captioned with glaring headlines promoting someone's agenda. When I take the time to read the article or watch the video I discover, almost invariably, the headline was purely, misleading B.S. – in other words: "Fake News." This, of course, indicates that the subsequent *Facebook* posters did not take the time to read or watch the article or video, but only shared it because they agreed with the glaring, B.S. headline – in other words: They just made themselves look like asses. Remember: Support assures us we are correct and *closes our minds.*

Furthermore, I have occasionally gone to the trouble of informing someone that they have been distributing false information, and they have taken offense to it. ("It's absolutely threatening to admit you're wrong.") Well, TOUGH COOKIES, if you want to dish it out learn how to take it!

I have even been told by some that they just forward all e-mails and share all *Facebook* posts from their "friends," without reading them first. Does this not epitomize gullibility? Dare I say, even stupidity?

Please, do yourself a favor, check it out or read it before you forward or share it. If you don't have time or you don't understand it then pass *on it* – don't pass *it on.* Keep in mind what Honest Abe Lincoln said: "Better to remain silent and be thought a fool than to speak out and remove all doubt."

That's quite a few ideas. As well as opinions, thoughts and facts to consider. But now we need to search deeper into what makes us, and those who endeavor to manipulate us, tick.

We will begin, in the next Chapter, with the idea that underlies and reinforces all the others. It is also the reason why demagogues – be they plutocrats, politicians or pundits – succeed or even exist.

VI

Prejudice: The Main Idea

It's All About That "Base"

Prejudice: "Preconceived opinion that is not based on reason or actual experience" (*Oxford Dictionary*)

In the previous chapter we learned that we all have a tendency to automatically accept wrong data, simply because it supports what we (already) believe, i.e., preconceived opinions. When those preconceived opinions aren't based on reason (common sense) or actual experience (personal encounter) they are biased, slanted or *prejudiced*. Those are the beliefs that are targeted by demagogues to convince us to act in their best interest and not our own.

Additionally, we learned, the speed at which demagogues bombard the prejudiced beliefs they target, through electronic media (TV), forces us to arrive at conclusions based on intuition instead of thought.

Therefore, since all propaganda appeals to our emotions (intuition), as opposed to our intellect (reasoned thought), if they catch us when we are gullible, unaware, or not thinking about what we're thinking, we are vulnerable.

The subject of prejudice is far from black and white (no pun intended). Psychologists and researchers have varied opinions, from extensive studies, about its origins and reasons. However, one fact is consistent, like propaganda, prejudice can be either positive or negative. When positive, prejudice reinforces our acceptance of those who are like us. But as my dad used to say: "There's good and bad in everything." When negative, prejudice reinforces our unwillingness to accept those who are different.

It is the negative aspect of prejudice that fogs up the positive side. There is an expression: "Fear of The Other." We tend to fear, or be suspicious of, or distrust, or resist accepting, those who are different, the other. Whatever makes another "the other," be it gender, race, religion, physical appearance, political philosophy, or a whole slew of things that might be different, flips our mental "radar" on. The good news is it's not our fault. Remember what Dr. Mark Goulston taught us (not that one – not now): Our brains are wired to jump to conclusions. Instinct uses past experience to make quick decisions, for the ultimate purpose of protecting us from harm. Furthermore, in his research on backfire, which causes us to hold onto our beliefs (prejudices) even after they have been proven incorrect, Professor Brendan Nyhan explained it as "a natural defense mechanism" because "it's absolutely threatening to admit you're wrong." Read on, there's more!

In his 1954 book on the subject, *The Nature of Prejudice*, Psychologist Gordon Allport (1897 – 1967) found prejudice to be part of a normal process for humans. According to him, our minds create categories to help us think. Thereby, we make prejudgments, based on the categories we create. This mental process is impossible to avoid. Our minds depend on it, to keep our lives in some kind of order. The CBS program *60 Minutes* televised a report about studies at Yale University which demonstrated this behavior in infants as young as three months. In other words, like Dr. Goulston says (no, not that one – not yet): Our brains are wired to rely on instinct – to make quick decisions.

In 1999, Marilynn Brewer, social psychologist and professor emeritus of psychology at Ohio State University, posited in her article "The Psychology of Prejudice: Ingroup Love and Outgroup Hate?" in *The Journal of Social Issues*, volume 55, issue 3 that we may create prejudice from positive feelings, like love and trust, we reserve for our ingroup – rather than hatred of the outgroup. [I]n other words, we like to root for our team, which is a manifestation of positive prejudice. (It's all about that BASE!)

But don't forget the flip side! If positive emotions are reserved for the ingroup it is then indicated they are denied from the outgroup. That leaves only indifference (at best) or negative emotions (at worst), either case would be a manifestation of negative prejudice. Taking Professor Brewer's theory through the chain of logic suggests that although (negative) prejudice may not come from hatred of the outgroup – hatred of outgroups may develop because of (positive) prejudice.

The double-edged sword of prejudice causes what psychologists call "cognitive dissonance." That is the anxiety felt when trying to justify having two or more conflicting ideas at the same time. In order to justify our own beliefs (positive prejudice), even after they might have been proven wrong, we need to justify our dislike of those who disagree or are somehow, otherwise "different" (negative prejudice). Remember what Mark Twain said: "A man cannot be comfortable without his own approval." It is cognitive dissonance that is at the root of backfire (or motivated reasoning). "Know-it-alls" cannot embrace conflicting ideas because "it's absolutely threatening to admit you're wrong." It is the understanding of the power of cognitive dissonance that allows demagogues to convince us to act against our own best interest, by telling us what we want to hear as opposed to what we need to hear.

On the subject of know-it-alls, Sociologist Theodor Adorno (1903 – 1969) theorized that an authoritarian personality led to prejudice. He defined these types as people who are inflexible in their thinking, and in obedience to figures of authority, and strictly follow rules and social order, as well as see everything as either all good or all bad. (The important thing to remember here is that not all those with authoritarian personalities are in positions of authority. Demagogues, with authority, know that anyone who will obey blindly, does not see there is good and bad in everything, and distrusts those who question "the rules" is the easiest person to manipulate.)

Allport defined prejudice as a good or bad perception of someone or something before having, or by ignoring, real knowledge. [I]n other words, from a standpoint of instinct. We understand, from Dr. Goulston, our brains are wired to jump to conclusions. Instinct relies on past experience. But past experience does not always possess all the knowledge needed to deal with present experience. That's why instinct is a shortcut, it's just a starting point, because instinct is often ignorant of new, relevant facts. Confucius said (yes, he really did): "Real knowledge is to know the extent of one's ignorance."

Ignorance is part of the human condition. Simply put, no one knows everything. Ignorance, in itself, is not a sin. Failure to accept one's ignorance is stupidity, which is.

When we are convinced to accept facts simply because they reinforce our prejudices, or worse yet, act on them (against our own best interests), we are acting through instinct and operating through ignorance. The antidote is to act through reason. Am I obeying blindly? Am I considering the bad as well as the good? Do the rules make sense (especially, for me)? In order to change – a mind must be open.

So how do we protect ourselves against being manipulated by appeals to our prejudices? (Yes – that one – now.) "THINK ABOUT WHAT YOU'RE THINKING."

VII

Plutocrats: The Inmates That Run the Asylum

"There is no great genius without some touch of madness." Aristotle

By now, you know I have a penchant for catchy titles. But this one is completely serious. In this essay, I will endeavor to demonstrate it with reason, logic and facts.

In the aftermath of the 2008 TARP (Troubled Asset Relief Program) bailout of Wall Street banks and investment firms, it came to light that some of the taxpayers' money given them was redirected to executive bonuses. Unsurprisingly, the CEO's responsible received widespread and vociferous criticism, including death threats. I remember one particular comment made by Missouri Senator Claire McCaskill. She called the CEO's of these companies "idiots." The term she chose was not exactly correct but it was pretty close. The actual truth is they are not stupid – they are insane.

On pages 104 – 106 of *Just Listen*, Dr. Mark Goulston describes the mentality of "psychopaths." One in every one-hundred people fit the mold. (If that number rings a bell, it should, because it equals [The] One-Percent!) Gratefully, not all of them become serial-killers. Psychiatrist Goulston commented that the dumb ones go to jail. The intelligent ones can become CEO's. Dr. Goulston explains that leaders in business benefit from psychopathic tendencies; lack of sympathy, narcissism, viciousness. He also warns that they will literally ruin your life, if it will aid them, with no remorse. He adds that it is impossible to make a psychopath have any genuine feeling for you. They can feign concern because they are natural con-artists. But in fact, they couldn't care less about anyone except themselves. Finally, he advises that they lack the mental tools to respond in any honest or principled way.

Dictionary.com defines psychopathy as a mental disorder in which an individual manifests amoral and antisocial behavior, lack of ability to love or establish meaningful personal relationships, extreme egocentricity, failure to learn from experience, etc. If CEO's using taxpayers' money, which was intended to fix a financial disaster of their own doing, to award themselves bonuses was not "amoral and antisocial behavior," "extreme egocentricity," and "failure to learn from experience" can someone please tell me what is?

In my essay examining "Big Government" in Chapter V, I referred to those with the psychotic desire to possess all property. In an interview she did on National Public Radio, on October 15, 2012, financial journalist and author of *Plutocrats*,

Chrystia Freeland, provided insight into how these psychotics are able to justify that sort of desire: They convince themselves that what's good for them is good for everyone. So, for example, cutting vital government programs is good because it lowers their taxes. (What Ms. Freeland uncovered here, through her interviews of many plutocrats, was cognitive dissonance, the need to justify their own beliefs and their dislike of those who disagree; *the other*.) Have you ever heard the expression "nobody in prison is guilty"? It's always someone else's fault. Remember what Mark Twain said: "A man cannot be comfortable without his own approval." That goes double for psychopaths.

Of course, not every plutocrat is a psychopath. That is, if the term is taken literally. *The Oxford Dictionary* defines plutocrat as "a person whose power derives from their wealth." Interpreted that way, anyone who uses their wealth to achieve power is a plutocrat, which would include virtually all of them, crazy or not. Indeed, there are some plutocrats who use their wealth to achieve power to do good. However, today the word plutocrat is used almost exclusively as a negative term (again, and as with the word propaganda, thanks mostly to Hitler). But for our purposes that's okay. In this dialogue, as with all the others in this book, we are (mostly) discussing the negative side, in order to determine how to protect ourselves against those who would do us harm. [O]r, more precisely, to protect ourselves against those who would manipulate us into harming ourselves, by convincing us to act against our own best interests. In order to do this we need to familiarize ourselves with the devices they employ.

One device is known as "The Expert Fallacy." Simply described, this is the phenomenon of accepting someone who presents the appearance of authority as being an actual authority. I learned about it by watching (history's greatest propaganda tool) television. Specifically, through a show on the National Geographic Channel entitled *Brain Games*. This series provides excellent insight into how our brains work, use shortcuts, and can be manipulated, in easy to understand, common-man language. (Don't forget, I'm only a high-school graduate!)

In their episode examining the "Power of Persuasion" they had an actor dressed in a suit and tie, accompanied by a "camera-man," ask random people ridiculous questions. People gladly entertained his questions because he presented himself as a legitimate reporter, an occupation perceived as an authority-figure or "expert." Have you ever witnessed pundits on TV using chalk-boards, or oversized legal pads, or power-point presentations displaying facts and/or statistics (often presented out of context) to back up their claims? Aren't they virtually always dressed in business-wear – the "uniform" of authority? Sometimes, not always but sometimes, they are employing "The Expert Fallacy." Always, not sometimes but always, they're claims should be examined, scrutinized and verified.

The Milgram experiment was, perhaps, the most famous examination of "The Expert Fallacy." It was performed at Yale University in the 1960's by psychologist Stanley Milgram, and replicated several times since. In it, the actual subject was given the impression that he/she was assisting an experimenter (the expert) in testing a "subject" (actually an actor). The subject was instructed to ask the "subject" questions, and administer electric shocks of increasing voltage for every incorrect answer (of course, the "shocks" were also an illusion). The actor-subject was in a separate room and could not be seen, only heard. As the "shocks" grew more intense, the actor would scream (as if) in pain. If the actual subject wanted to stop the experiment, out of concern for the "subject's" life, he/she was told by the "expert" to proceed.

In the original experiment and all replications, the results were found to be consistent – 61% to 66% of the actual subjects – when encouraged by the "expert" – were willing to go all the way.

Milgram wrote an article about his experiment for Harper's Magazine in 1974 – in it he stated that when his subjects' sense of morality was challenged by authority, even as their victims screamed, they capitulated most of the time. Average people, just performing their work, with no thought of malice, can be made to act viciously. Furthermore, even when their viciousness becomes evident, but they are instructed to continue to do work that goes against their morals, by a figure of authority, very few are able to resist.

CEO's are figures of authority, just because they're CEO's, and they know it. They also know all about phenomena, like "The Expert Fallacy," and the credibility they gain from them, earned or not. They know about Milgram's experiment, and that it showed 61% to 66% of people, which is a landslide, are willing to kill just because they are told to by a figure of authority. And, if they don't know about this stuff, they employ people to know about this stuff – and to use it to help them get their way. Remember, they're insane not stupid!

Another method plutocrats employ to get their way is simply manipulating "the system," in a wide variety of ways. One is bribery (in America we call it lobbying) of politicians. Creative accounting is another device. They employ expert (and very creative) accountants and lawyers to take advantage of loopholes in the laws, particularly the tax laws. That is how GE, for example, made $14.2 billion in 2010 and paid "no" tax. Of course, the loopholes exist in the first place because the plutocrats lobbied the politicians to put them there.

Plutocrats also manipulate the system by employing the strategy of "if you can't beat them – join them." One example is Jeffrey Immelt, CEO of GE and head of President Obama's Economic Recovery Advisory Board. He's the guy who oversaw GE's elimination of twenty percent of its American workers.

Another is Henry Paulson, CEO of Goldman-Sachs from 1999 to 2006 and United States Secretary of the Treasury from 2006 to 2009. Paulson orchestrated the TARP bailout, by which Goldman-Sachs benefitted greatly – although – the company made a substantial profit from the causational, financial crisis (that it helped bring about) by "short-selling" subprime mortgage backed securities. Some Goldman-Sachs executives were advisors to Paulson, others had moved on to additional companies that benefitted from TARP. The "Assistant Secretary of the Treasury for Financial Stability" – the guy responsible for handing out the TARP funds – was Neel Kashkari, a former vice-president at Goldman Sachs.

Henry Paulson's predecessor, as Goldman-Sachs's CEO, was Jon Corzine. When he left the company, Corzine became a U.S. Senator from, and then Governor of, New Jersey. During his term as Governor his approval rating consistently dropped and he was the only Governor in the state's history to have a recall (although it failed) initiated against him. After his term as Governor ended, in 2010, Corzine once again became a CEO, of MF Global, a bond and futures brokerage company. Also in 2010, he was a partner of J.C. Flowers & Company, an investment firm, which was founded by another Goldman-Sachs alumnus, J.C. Flowers. The Flowers Company held 10% ownership of MF Global. In 2011, MF Global declared bankruptcy.

Subsequently, the Commodity Futures Trading Commission brought a civil lawsuit against Corzine for using customer funds for corporate purposes. Presently, Corzine has not been formally charged with committing any crime and, it is rumored, he is planning to open a hedge fund. Gary Gensler, still another graduate of Goldman-Sachs, is the present (at the time of this writing) Chairman of (you guessed it) the Commodity Futures Trading Commission.

Robert Rubin was with Goldman-Sachs for twenty-six years. After that he worked in the Clinton administration. First, as Director of the National Economic Council, this was created by President Clinton. Then he became United States Secretary of the Treasury from 1995 to 1999, also under Clinton. As Treasury Secretary, Rubin prevented the regulation of credit derivatives, with the help of Federal Reserve Chairman Alan Greenspan (Brown Brothers Harriman [investment bank], J.P. Morgan & Company, Mobil Corporation, among others). With the help of his deputy and successor, Lawrence Summers (former World Bank Chief Economist – one of his theories is that Unemployment insurance leads to unemployment), Rubin also got the Glass–Steagall Act of 1933 abrogated. Both actions are considered "major contributing factors" in the 2008 financial crisis. After leaving government in 1999 Robert Rubin held several high positions with Citigroup through 2009. During his tenure, Citigroup paid him $126 million. In 2008 – 2009 Citigroup received the largest TARP bailout of any financial institution.

Then there is Donald Trump. His "extreme egocentricity," "failure to learn from experience," narcissism, selfishness, callousness, natural persuasiveness, and other psychopathic traits, are well accounted by many who know him. They are also obvious to many who simply observe him. He got elected President by promising to "drain the swamp" of Washington D.C.'s bureaucracy. Then he proceeded to fill the swamp with alligators, like a Secretary of Education who does not believe in Public Education; five Goldman-Sachs alumni, including (again) a Secretary of the Treasury; and an EPA Administrator who sued the EPA fourteen times!

By getting laws passed to favor *them* – preventing and repealing laws that might limit their profits – coercing the government into bailing them out when their plans get out of hand – getting themselves and their cronies into high places – convincing politicians (and many of *us*) they can't create any jobs unless their taxes are lowered – while – they are paying "no" tax and still cutting American jobs – are plutocrats demonstrating they're psychopaths, without conscience? [O]r are these just a series of unfortunate coincidences?

I know what I think. I am concerned about what others think. And I am worried about those (of *us*) who don't stop to think.

VIII

Atlas Masturbates: The Acolytes of Ayn Rand and Their Self Serving Circle-jerk

Be kind to the people you meet on the way up – because you're gonna meet the same people – on the way down

In 1957, the book *Atlas Shrugged* by Ayn Rand (1905 – 1982) was published. In it, Rand describes a dystopian United States of America in which a corrupt government "loots" the most intelligent and successful citizens, by way of unfair taxes and regulations, in order to provide for "moochers" (the poor). The plot revolves around a scheme by "the great minds" to go on strike. Thereby demonstrating that, without them, the world could not function. The book's title is a metaphor for the scheme, i.e., if Atlas were to shrug the world would fall. (Just as a side note, the image of Atlas carrying the world is actually incorrect. Atlas, in Greek mythology, was compelled to hold up "the heavens.")

Atlas Shrugged is, of course, a novel. The problem is that Rand's acolytes see it as biblical. They believe, as Rand did herself, the philosophies she explores through the story should be taken as gospel, to live by.

The gospel of Ayn Rand visits ideas such as "the virtue of selfishness" (the title for another one of her works) and "the destructiveness of altruism." When explained, her ideas do not appear to be as monstrous as they sound at first blush. According to Rand, selfishness (as a virtue) refers to self-value and self-reliance, and altruism is seen as destructive because it places value on others "before" oneself. Furthermore, she advised that one should espouse her philosophies with "morality, honesty and justice." John Galt, the main character of *Atlas Shrugged,* lives by an "oath" that summarizes the philosophy of Ayn Rand. Galt's (Rand's) oath declares that he will never live his life for someone else's well-being or ask anyone to live for his.

It all sounds very high-minded, but only for a novel. In the real world it's merely mental-masturbation, due to the nature of mankind. Rand, ostensibly, had great regard for facts, truth, reason and logic. With that in mind, let us give the philosophy of Ayn Rand and her acolytes the "Judge Judy Test" (Does it make sense?). Were she alive today, Rand would, my guess is, probably not approve.

The premise of *Atlas Shrugged* simply boils down to one idea: Prosperity is created by the mind. For example, Henry Ford created prosperity with his idea of the assembly line. The men and women who worked on his assembly line benefitted from his idea. In the real world that is undeniably a reasonable fact, logical and true. However, the reverse is also true. If Henry Ford did not employ other men and women to produce a product, his idea, by itself, could not have created prosperity for anyone – including him.

Rand addresses this truth in her book through one of the characters, the owner of a steel mill. Because he demands the best workforce, he pays wages that are significantly higher than any union scale in the nation. The workers at the steel mill are also unionized, albeit through a "company union," which is usually powerless and only for show. But in this (fictional) case, the union membership (the workers) is apparently treated with respect and equality. In the real world, however, this is almost never the case.

In the real world "the great minds" fight tooth-and-nail to prevent workers from unionizing, in order to pay them lower wages. More often than not, rather than appreciating the fact that it takes two to tango, like the imaginary plutocrat of *Atlas Shrugged* does, real world plutocrats (remember, we are talking about the evil kind) conveniently forget this fact of life. They conceptualize the premise of *Atlas Shrugged* to infer that they are better than those they employ. Consequently, they feel their workers should be glad to have a job and only need to be paid enough to eat, i.e., remain alive, and afford carfare to get to work. An example was, again, Henry Ford.

Ford (the company) was the last of the "Big Three" American automakers to unionize. During the workforce demonstrations for unionization at Ford, Henry Ford employed gangsters (and that is not just an expression, like thug or goon, these were bona fide, organized criminals) to attack his employees. Ford did not capitulate to negotiations with the United Automobile Workers until the union's President, the great Walter Reuther, was beaten to a pulp and courageously refused to be taken to a hospital until news photographers could capture images of his injuries. Only then, after the public embarrassment of those pictures, showing what "the great minds" were capable of, did Ford finally decide to espouse the philosophies of "morality, honesty and justice."

Another example of Rand's philosophy, which she coined "objectivism," taken to the extreme, was postulated by Leonard Peikoff. We explored his idea that "Healthcare is not a right" in Chapter V. Peikoff was one of Ayn Rand's direct disciples and is also heir to her estate. After her death, he founded the Ayn Rand Institute.

Alan Greenspan – who as Federal Reserve Chairman aided Treasury Secretary Robert Rubin in deregulating banks, helping to cause the 2008 mortgage crisis – was a personal friend and associate of Ayn Rand. As such, he along with her other confidants, read the book *Atlas Shrugged* as it was being written.

Atlas Shrugged is sort of a "bible" for the Tea Party movement. At Tea Party rallies, shirts and signs can be seen emblazoned with the slogan "I am John Galt."

Rick Santelli, the CNBC reporter who "ranted" that certain people were "losers" because *they were cheated* by dishonest mortgage brokers, is a self-proclaimed "Ayn Rander." He also promoted the idea of holding a "Chicago Tea Party" to protest Government attempts to give the "losers" any relief.

Senator Ted Cruz, of Texas, quoted *Atlas Shrugged* in his twenty-four hour filibuster attempting to have the Affordable Care Act ("Obama-Care") repealed. The ACA had already become law, and had been upheld by the Supreme Court. Therefore, at the time, the Senator's filibuster was recognized as simple, self-indulgent grandstanding, as well as for being a principle cause of the consequential Government shutdown. But, of course, Cruz and his cohorts haven't given up and have learned nothing from "past experience." The Tea Party is known to heavily support Senator Cruz.

Congressman Paul Ryan, of Wisconsin, advocates reducing taxes for the wealthiest citizens and for corporations, some of which already pay "none." He also urges cutting Medicare, Medicaid, Pell Grants, food stamps and low-income housing.

Social Security was declared by Ryan to be a "socialist-based system" in a speech he gave to a group of Ayn Rand devotees. All of these programs help either the indigent or the middle class. (Simultaneously, Ryan takes every opportunity to proclaim himself a champion of the middle class.) Speaking at a celebration for what would have been Ayn Rand's 100th birthday, Paul Ryan said he entered "public service" because of her. In the same address, he said that he requires his interns and staff to read the works of Ayn Rand. He once told the *Weekly Standard*, in a 2003 interview, he gave copies of *Atlas Shrugged* out as Christmas gifts. Like Sen. Ted Cruz, Rep. Paul Ryan is heavily supported by the Tea Party.

One final revelation – about Paul Ryan's "values" – in 2012, when nominated to run for Vice-President, a position with a much bigger voter base in which the Tea Party is a minority – he claimed that his devotion to Ayn Rand, who inspired him to enter public service, was just an "urban legend." He added that, as a Catholic, he found Thomas Aquinas* (whose teachings are the basis for the idea of Social Justice) more influential. (*Note to "Ayn Rand Scholar" Paul Ryan: Rand claimed, with characteristic immodesty, besides herself only two other philosophers "mattered," Aristotle and *Aquinas*.)

Ayn Rand has John Galt express another viewpoint in the book, which describes her philosophy much more accurately than his aforementioned oath. Galt (Rand) proclaims that those "at the top" give everything to those "at the bottom" and receive nothing in return. Furthermore, Rand writes, those at the bottom have nothing of value to offer to the great minds who are their superiors and would be helpless and go hungry, if left to themselves.

Appreciative, considerate and modest as Galt may be (you are correct, I'm being sarcastic) he is not my "favorite" (yes, I'm being sarcastic again) *Atlas Shrugged* character. That would be a guy named Ragnar with some kind of

Scandinavian last name that I won't bother with because my keyboard can't make umlauts. Ragnar is a brilliant philosopher who becomes a pirate. (Of course he does! It happens all the time!) He's a reverse Robin Hood that robs from the poor ("the parasites") and gives to the rich ("the producers"). (As we learned in Chapter I, this is called "regressive income redistribution.")

That's enough setup – time to call in "Judge Judy"!

Does Ayn Rand's philosophy make sense? Well, I would say, no and yes. No – if you're a human being. Yes – if you're a selfish louse that doesn't want to pay your taxes and thinks you deserve a free ride on the backs of everyone who didn't go as far as you did in school. Vulgar, and correct, as that may be, it is, however, oversimplification. We need to delve deeper into this "philosophy," and especially into how it is used to convince us "parasites" to act against our own best interests.

First, consider Rand's use of language. If you want to encourage "self-value and self-reliance" why not just say that – like Thomas Aquinas did? Why, instead, characterize and glorify those admirable traits as "the virtue of selfishness"? The only reason can logically be that one wants to encourage certain people to think of them selves as better than certain others (the propaganda technique of appeal to prejudice). The same (appeal to prejudice) goes for her description of altruism as "destructive" because it places value on others "before" oneself. Imagine if Jonas Salk had shared Rand's opinion of altruism. What if, instead of refusing to have his discovery of the polio vaccine patented, he'd decided to hold out for the highest bidder? Think of how "destructive" that could have been.

Ayn Rand, as well as her acolytes, extolled capitalism, and especially Laissez-faire (unregulated) capitalism, as the only "just" economic system. The financial crisis of 2008 demonstrated the destructiveness of "the great minds" when freed from regulations. Furthermore, her opinion of thinkers, "at the top," as the only producers and those, "at the bottom," who do the production, as "parasites," is more akin to Communism (not the theoretical kind but the failed, real-world kind).

It's easy to understand how the appeal to prejudice in *Atlas Shrugged*, with its selective "facts," self-serving "truth," lopsided "reason" and twisted "logic," could embolden those with selfish and egotistical tendencies, "at the top," to feel superior. But how can they use it to convince those of us "at the bottom" to act against our own best interests? It's because we have the same selfish and egotistical tendencies. The fascination is in how they take advantage of that through propaganda. Our defense is in understanding how that propaganda takes advantage of our selfish and egotistical tendencies.

We already understand. It's by accepting, so-called, "facts" because they reinforce our beliefs, without thinking about what we're thinking. So let's think about it.

Despite her claims of devotion to reason, Ayn Rand's philosophy, as presented in *Atlas Shrugged*, appeals to the emotions (instinct and intuition) not the intellect (reason). That is propaganda. Specifically, it's appeal to prejudice propaganda. Her followers will, of course, call me mistaken (or probably worse). They will argue that it's intellectual.

When the "facts" in *Atlas Shrugged* are truthfully considered, with reason and logic, they are revealed to be intellectualized propaganda.

Atlas Shrugged is a novel. It is a fairy tale. It is a cock-and-bull-story, created to foment fear of the other. Namely, the fear the Haves bear toward the Have-Nots. The way they get us "parasites" to act against our own best interests is to create another *other* for *us* to fear.

We discussed, in Chapter V, the fact that Americans, almost universally, despise paying taxes. Very few of us care to suck it up and accept taxes as a necessary fact of civilized life. The "producers" (plutocrats and the politicians and pundits they employ) parasitically prey on us "parasites" by convincing the unaware and unthinking in our ranks that there are worse parasites, at the bottom of "the bottom," who are selfishly benefitting from our tax dollars, without contributing to society. (That brings up an interesting contradiction to consider. If those "at the top" are so anti-socialist and only value the individual, why are they so concerned about anyone's failure to contribute to society?) They attack Entitlement programs such as Unemployment, Medicare, Medicaid, Pell Grants, food stamps, low-income housing and Social Security as "handouts," in order to convince those of us who "should be glad to have a job" that we need to side with them, because they will "protect" us from having our pockets picked by these programs. The ultimate irony is that all those of us lucky enough to have a job may need to take advantage of one or more of these programs from time to time.

So the plutocrat parasites spread the idea that they are our friends and we have a common enemy. We must side with them to protect ourselves from the "moochers" who are beneath *even us!* But by what ways do they spread their idea? They spread it in plenty of ways – and incessantly.

Remember our discussion about "Social Media" in Chapter V? My motivation to write that was not just because I'm tired of videos of cats knocking over flower pots. It was because social media is one of the most effective of all propaganda tools. To this day, I still see e-mails and *Facebook* posts proclaiming President Obama a Socialist (pejoratively) as well as a non-citizen. I see out-of-context "facts" and twisted "logic" employed, attempting to convince the uninformed to hate certain *others*. And these e-mails and posts obviously do not originate from some guy with nothing else to do on a Saturday night. They are crafted and calculated to prey on the unaware, the uninformed, and those not thinking about what they're thinking. Then, what do *we* do? We "share" them, without verifying or, often, even reading more than their headlines, first.

Radio and, of course, (history's greatest propaganda tool) television are employed relentlessly. Through their dissolute demagogue, pundit puppets – such as Rush Limbaugh, almost everyone on FNC, and other extremists – plutocrat-parasites spread their appeal to prejudice. Then, what do *we* do? We go to social media and "share" the propaganda we hear on radio or see on TV.

Finally, and most destructively, the politicians in the pockets of plutocrats are not only spreading their malevolent message but also enacting their diabolical dogma. Subversive Senator Ted Cruz shows no remorse at all for the Government shutdown he helped bring about, or for the disastrous harm it caused. How can that be? It's because, as a subversive, Cruz's goal is the permanent shutdown of government, he even brags about it. Although, he characterizes himself as a patriot – not a subversive – actions speak louder than words, let's call a spade a spade. And regarding the harm he caused, as an "Ayn Rander," to harm – not help – is his sworn goal. Let the "parasites" eat cake, or even better, each other!

The irony is that, if they succeed in abolishing government, where else could slobs like Ted Cruz and Paul Ryan find a job? Their plutocrat, puppet-masters will most likely care for them. But for the rest of us it would be like the, pre-union, Ford Motor Company – even like Communist (insert name of your most hated former Communist nation here.)

The Tea Party movement, too, was a brilliant scheme by plutocrats to be a perfect path to pollute patriotism. As ultra-Conservatives, members of the Tea Party were the most likely to be people who are inflexible in their thinking and in obedience to figures of authority, and strictly follow rules and social order, as well as see everything as either all good or all bad. [I]n other words, the easiest types of persons to manipulate. And, besides the Tea Party, there are many more (let's hope not too many) of us who fall into the same ideological category. So once the Tea Party was identified for its potential to be used, plutocrats poured in the money, politicians and pundits. The next step was to find *the other* (that would be the "losers" who pick the pockets of us hard working, middle class "parasites") for them to convince us to fear and hate.

The dog-eat-dog attitude we see on the ultra-Right today, making a mockery of our system of government and convincing many of us to fight amongst ourselves, brings to mind three great quotations: Demosthenes, "A man is his own easiest dupe, for what he wishes to be true he generally believes to be true." (Unless he thinks about what he's thinking.) Henry David Thoreau, "It's never too late to give up your prejudices." (But you only will once you realize they only hurt *you*.) And finally, George Santayana, "Those who cannot remember the past are condemned to repeat it." (What I want to add, about this one, is hard to say. BUT FOR GOD'S SAKE – it's as plain as the nose on your face! Anyone who does not believe that America can be taken over by those who endeavor to convince us to act against our own best interests need only remember the past. Specifically [again – this is obvious – but very hard to say] – Hitler – who convinced an entire nation of people that he was their savior and turned out to be their enslaver, by finding an *other* [that would be the Jews] for them to fear and hate.)

That brings us, again, to Donald Trump – who stacked-the-deck by targeting *several* "others", who he convinced many of us to fear and hate – proving that "those who cannot remember the past are condemned to repeat it."

IX

Conservunism

"Under capitalism, man exploits man. Under communism, it's just the opposite."

John Kenneth Galbraith

I coined the term "conservunism," a combination of conservatism and communism, to illustrate how the Atlas-Masturbators are jerking followers into acting against their own best interests.

Patrick J. Buchanan, in *Where the Right Went Wrong*, excoriates neo-conservatives (by name) for "subverting" the conservative ideology, in general, and the Republican Party, specifically. As a staunch, some would say ultra, Conservative, Buchanan blames the neo-cons for hijacking the "Reagan Revolution." And he characterizes them as Liberals in Conservative costumes. It's not surprising that, with his firm belief in and defense of Conservatism, Mr. Buchanan would see subversives as Liberal infiltrators. Whether he's correct or not doesn't really matter. Be they (ostensibly) Conservatives, Liberals, Republicans or Democrats, these subversives are opportunists with their own agenda.

Having been an advisor to three Republican Presidents – Nixon, Ford and Reagan, as well as a presidential candidate himself – Buchanan, whether staunch or ultra in his beliefs, has viewed the nation and the world, for many years, from the top. However, it has been demonstrated repeatedly to those of us at the bottom as well, Pat Buchanan is correct in his assertion that it's the Right, generally, and the Republican Party, specifically, which has been infiltrated by these opportunistic "neo-commies" (my word, not his). What is even more revealing about his conviction is the fact that when he ran in the national election, excluding two Republican primaries, for President, Mr. Buchanan did so with the Reform Party. Founded by Ross Perot, the Reform Party has endorsed candidates as diverse as Perot himself, Ralph Nader, Pat Buchanan and Jesse Ventura, who won the governorship of Minnesota in 1998. Upon returning to the Republican Party, Buchanan has called today's G.O.P. what they got into government to "run out of town." He has also characterized both major parties, Democratic and Republican, as having become hardly dissimilar.

Jesse Ventura, addressing the same theme, voiced the belief that all political parties, if successful, will become "corrupt." In the event he runs for office again, Ventura has stated he will do so as an Independent.

The important question for *us* to consider, regarding the observations of both Buchanan and Ventura, is: What makes party politics corrupt? Of course, the answer is MONEY! Remember that politicians are only interested in two things – "votes and contributions" – and that the big-money hedges the bet by contributing equally to both sides. Therefore, their agenda is to protect their jobs – not *our* interests, which are why we vote for who we vote for. The obvious answer is for us to stop playing "follow the leader." As long as we continue to vote for politicians, obligated to special interests, big-money, and their own agenda, just because they tell us what we want to hear, through clever propaganda, we will continue to sabotage our own best interests.

Only when enough of us "average" Americans find the courage to vote for truly, *independent representatives* (not politicians) – whose only agenda is public service – will we begin to purge the saboteurs and subversives from politics.

In my view, from the bottom, Jesse Ventura's position of supporting unaffiliated, independent representatives as being the best means of avoiding corruption makes the most sense. However, Patrick J. Buchanan deserves credit for his position as well.

Whether one agrees with Pat Buchanan's views or not, they are palpably sincere and reflect his love for his country. Furthermore, by going back to his beloved Republican Party and speaking out against the direction in which he sees it headed requires tremendous courage, as well as open-mindedness. Remember what we learned in our study of prejudice, in Chapter VI, it's hard-wired into our nature to root for those who (supposedly) agree with us – our team. Critical examination of our team-mates takes independence, and calling them "subversive" takes fortitude. Patrick J. Buchanan deserves to be commended, not only for being courageous in his thinking, but also for thinking about what he's thinking.

Where I tend to diverge with Buchanan, in addition to his staunch Conservatism, is in the belief that his Republican Party can somehow be saved.

For that matter, the Democratic Party also seems beyond salvation. Politicians from both major parties are now, and have been for a long time, only interested in keeping their jobs – not doing their jobs. That's why someone like Paul Ryan, as an example, panders to his Tea Party constituency at the local level but when cast onto the national stage, tempers his "convictions" to appeal to a broader base.

In his book, Pat Buchanan describes neo-cons as former "liberals, leftists, socialists" and even "ex-Trotskyites," who began drifting over to the Republican Party when (their) Democratic Party began to lose its taste for war, toward the end of the Vietnam conflict. Apparently, he is correct. It's documented.

However, if Buchanan is also correct, which, again, he apparently is, in observing that the Democratic and Republican Parties are now hardly dissimilar, what difference does it make?

That brings us back to the concept of "Conservunism."

What's in a name? We can call the subversives that Patrick J. Buchanan fears the most "neo-conservatives," "neo-cons" (I like that one. It's not only short for conservative, it's also short for con-artist.), "neo-commies" or "conservunists." They are all wolves in sheep's clothing. The reason they drifted to the Republican Party is because of their understanding of prejudice. They know that the party's conservative base traditionally embraces their "moral values" in a way that makes them easier to sway. (We will learn more about that in the next chapter.) Let us begin our logical, reasonable and factual analysis on that side of the aisle.

Ronald Reagan, the beloved "patron saint" of the Republican Party, was a COMMUNIST!

I'll leave that last sentence as a separate paragraph, so it's easier for those who are ready to kill me to take out of context. For those of us who are more interested in facts, read on.

The Reagan Revolution, mourned by Pat Buchanan for having been "hijacked" by the Conservunists, was more akin to the Bolshevik Revolution. And Ronald Reagan was the Father of Conservunism. As a trained actor, which was all he really was, Reagan was the perfect stooge for the commies in conservative costumes to make the shill in their con-game. And ever since Reagan's reprehensible reign, those of us "at the bottom" have been fighting to claw our way out of the ashes.

In the late 1940's, Reagan, and his (then) wife, Jane Wyman, secretly supplied the FBI with the names of people in the entertainment industry "they believed were Communist sympathizers." The Bureau even gave Reagan a code name: "Informant T-10." (*Time* magazine: September 9, 1985)

During this period, Reagan was President of the Screen Actors Guild, which means he ratted out his "friends" and constituents he had sworn to serve. He did this, not because he had evidence they were Communist sympathizers, but because he "believed" they were. In other words, they disagreed with his politics, which the First Amendment of The United States Constitution protects their right to. It was noted that Reagan expressed slight disdain. But he ratted anyway. Of course, when approached by the FBI, he had the option, as his second wife famously advised, to "Just Say No!" His more courageous – and less ambitious – colleagues did.

(The thing to keep in mind about Conservunists is they are always ultra-anti-Communists – in name. But at the same time, they are practical Communists – in their theories, beliefs, tactics and methods.)

Reagan started out in politics as a member of the Democratic Party. During the 1950s, the plutocrats at the General Electric Company began his grooming while he was their TV spokesman. From them, he learned to embrace the philosophies of free (meaning regulation free) markets, small government (one that minds its own business) and anti-unionism (the marginalization of workers). In 1962, when his TV ratings began to decline, GE dumped him. In that same year, well before the other Conservunists followed him, he switched over to the Republican Party.

As Governor of California, Reagan sent in the Highway Patrol to break up protests at UC Berkeley in 1969. After the death of a student and the blinding of a bystander, he sent in the National Guard as well. When asked about protesters – a year later – Reagan said he would not appease them, even if it meant a "bloodbath." Thus shamelessly disregarding the First Amendment's guarantee of "... the right of the people peaceably to assemble, and to petition the Government for a redress of grievances."

On his first day as President of The United States of America, in his inauguration speech, Reagan unveiled the mantra that would become his trademark, "... government is not the solution to our problems; government is the problem." (If that's how you feel about government – why work in government – unless your goal is to dismantle the Government?) Then – Ronald Reagan got to work – fighting Communism and steering America toward Conservunism.

Halfway through his first year as President, 1981, Reagan got a gift that started the ball rolling. PATCO, the Professional Air Traffic Controllers Union (which, by the way, supported Reagan in his run for President), went on strike in violation of federal law. Cleverly, Reagan used federal law against them. Declaring a national emergency, he gave them 48 hours to return to work or else forfeit their jobs. Stupidly, the union's leadership advised, and nearly all the membership agreed, they call his bluff. The outcome was that all the striking workers were fired as promised.

Moreover, by foolishly not living to fight another day, when all odds were against them, PATCO gave the Conservunist movement its opening to wage war on American workers. Not only did Reagan's tactics break a powerful, albeit arrogant, labor union, it emboldened plutocrats to use similar tactics, both legal and illegal, to destroy hard-fought workplace fairness throughout the land.

Reagan further helped his dear plutocrat-providers' cause with his appointments to the National Labor Relations Board. The Board was traditionally composed of impartial members – until Reagan. He appointed John Van de Water, a management consultant who orchestrated union busting campaigns – Donald Dotson, a corporate labor counsel – and Robert Hunter, aide to anti-union Senator Orrin Hatch.

Remember what Pat Buchanan said in his book, which I first mentioned in Chapter V? Global American companies now want, expect and get tremendous tax incentives, government subsidies, authorization to bring foreign workers here because they can pay them less, free-rein to send their manufacturing plants and jobs outside U.S. borders and the freedom to import their own products back here without tariffs to be sold to American citizens, as credit for their contributions to our elected representatives. Buchanan is correct in those observations, and they have only gotten worse since the reign of Reagan. However, he is incorrect in the defense of his beloved, former boss. We have Reagan's policy of "Trickle Down Economics" to thank for the conditions Buchanan observed. Reagan advocated lowering taxes on corporations and the wealthy, as well as the Laissez-faire policy. The neo-cons did not hijack the Reagan Revolution – Reagan led the revolution. Buchanan also said, in the same book; free market capitalists believe whatever is best for them is best for the USA, which isn't conservatism. On that point, Pat's correct again.

It's *Conservunism* – communism disguised as conservatism – and Ronald Reagan was the movement's "Vladimir Lenin"!

During his 1980 presidential campaign, Reagan gave a rousing, flag-waving propaganda laced speech, in the shadow of the Statue of Liberty. It was Labor Day. And on that day, Ronald Reagan bamboozled many of us into believing he was our man. Some of the things he said were that he was the only union president ever to run for U.S. President (leaving out, of course, how he stabbed his union's members in the back). He promised to hear and address workers' needs. He brilliantly invoked "spiritual and moral values." He praised the Solidarity (Union), fighting their (Communist) State oppressors in Poland. He proclaimed that there is no freedom without free unionism. AND – He promised to "make America great again," in those exact words. Do they ring a bell? Then he became the Plutocrat-Puppet President of the United States of America.

Since the Democratic and Republican Parties are now hardly dissimilar, let's move to the Left side of the aisle. NAFTA, the North American Free Trade Agreement, was signed by Democratic President Bill Clinton. Its destructiveness is outlined well in Pat Buchanan's book. The only people it aided were the plutocrats who pushed Clinton to approve it. Democratic President Obama's proposed Free Trade agreement would, most likely, have been equally destructive. Clinton also repealed Glass-Steagall.

Conservunism has no affiliation and only one interest – the self. Be it by plutocrats who would rather employ Mexican workers at $20 a day instead of Americans at $20 an hour – or by politicians, of either major party, who are more interested in "votes and contributions" than in protecting Americans.

Communism is based on the one party or ruling party system. In Conservunist America, the plutocrats are the ruling party. Their control over both the Democratic and Republican Parties, with their contributions and influence, has relegated our two party system to irrelevance. The only way to correct this is to quit being "team" players and put our own best interests first, like the plutocrats do. Voting for Independent representatives, who refuse to be bought, is how "we shall overcome!"

That brings us, once again, to Donald Trump. As my dad used to say, there's good and bad in everything. Getting elected because he was seen as "independent" and not a "team player," demonstrates that America is ready to elect a *truly* Independent candidate. I'd like to see a serious third party (or should we say, a "second" [?]) started, with sincere representatives that refuse special-interest-contributions. An alternative political party, made up of (current) Independents, as well as any Democrats and Republicans with the courage to say enough is enough, it appears, can finally succeed. A party that refuses to be bought by the oligarchy and makes their job "doing their job" instead of "keeping their job," or getting rich, is the way to really make America great again! What do *you* think?

X

The State of the Unions' Distress

"For the strength of the pack is the wolf, and the strength of the wolf is the pack." Rudyard Kipling

"YOU ARE THE UNION!" I can't begin to count how many times I have heard that said, or said it myself as a union representative, to a union member. Whenever union members complain they are not getting "their way" they are, not often enough, reminded of that.

Every January, the President of the United States presents what is known as "The State of the Union Address." Many of us tend to forget that, as American citizens, we are all members of a "union." As union members our duty (to ourselves) is the insistence upon fair treatment for all members. This is because, as Adam Smith said, a society cannot be peaceful or successful when most members are impoverished and unhappy. And the reason to concern ourselves with the welfare of all our members, in order to ensure our own peace and success, is because nothing is more dangerous to society than someone with "nothing to lose," as James Baldwin said.

But I digress. My focus in this chapter is the distress of our labor unions. As Ronald Reagan said, without free unionism there is no freedom. Of course, he only said it as lip service to get elected. However, nothing more true was ever spoken.

I won't go into any detailed history of labor unions in America. That's easy enough to look up if you're interested. But I do want to remind those who might have forgotten, the Labor Union movement is responsible for many of the pleasures we sometimes take for granted. For instance, we enjoy the 40 hour work week, vacation time, medical benefits and pensions because others fought and in some cases died for them – for *us*. That is, also, easy enough to look up.

When I worked as a Media Specialist in the Air Transport Division of the Transport Workers Union of America, the folks who occasionally bring New York City to a halt with a transit strike (That would be Local 100, the union's largest Local, which knows how to keep and use its power!), I traveled around the country and visited many different Locals. As a videographer, part of my job was to interview members for informational videos. Invariably, at least one member at every Local would ask me the same question: "Can I work here without paying union dues?" Of course, my answer was always the same: "NO!"

Some union members see dues as an expense. In truth, it is insurance. Some people, who work at non-union jobs, are anti-union because they don't enjoy the same benefits and working conditions as union workers. If you feel that way, why not join (or form) a union? Well, there are several reasons.

One reason is that it's easier to be jealous and take what's offered as opposed to the effort involved in unionizing. Other reasons stem from employer tactics.

Some employers will use scare tactics and misinformation promoting, for instance, the myth that union dues will be an expense that will reduce workers' salaries. In fact, union workers are paid anywhere from 10% to 30% higher salaries (that's easy enough to look up, too). Employers will also threaten to fire, or just fire, workers suspected of attempting to unionize. By the way, both of the above employer tactics are illegal.

Anti-union employers are, to put it simply, penny-pinching plutocrats. [O]r in some cases, penny-pinching, *wannabe* plutocrats. They don't see the big picture. They fail to realize that a union benefits not only the worker, but the employer as well. That is, a smart employer.

In my travels, I not only interviewed union members but their employers as well, at major airlines, military bases and even Cape Canaveral. The workers at "The Cape" who clean and maintain the buildings, feed and cloth the astronauts, operate the rescue equipment and also launch the rockets are all Transport Workers Union members. The smart managers I spoke with appreciated how much the union made their jobs easier. They told me that when a discrepancy might arise, having a union committee to sit down with to nip it in the bud was a blessing. They told me that when an employee had to be disciplined, having a set of agreed-upon guidelines made a distasteful task bearable. And every single manager told me they appreciated the fact that, because the union workforce got better pay, they got better pay.

But to a psychopath, fairness is a foreign concept. Plutocrats, with their unwavering desire to have it all, are the main reason for the decline of union membership to an all time low, as well as the general frowning upon of unions.

Pro-plutocrat Conservunists in Congress enacted the 1947 Taft-Hartley Act, which greatly diminished the benefits of the earlier (1935) Wagner Act, which established law protecting the right to unionize and collectively bargain with employers. To date, all attempts to repeal the Taft-Hartley act have failed.

In the twenty-first century, the Employee Free Choice Act was an attempt to amend the Wagner Act, to gain back some of the protections lost through the Taft-Hartley Act. Opponents of the EFCA cite its provision of certifying a union based upon a majority of workers having signed union certification cards (referred to as "card check") as un-democratic. As the law stands now, even if all workers at a facility indicate they favor a union, an employer can insist upon an additional "secret ballot." Through cunning propaganda, Conservunist plutocrats, politicians and pundits portrayed the card check clause as un-American. By cleverly playing with words, they implied that denying the "secret ballot" denied the worker the right to privacy in his vote. They contended that allowing for card check elections (only) would allow everyone to know how everyone else voted. I have personally voted in several card check elections. They are always done by mail and must be returned in double, sealed envelopes. Card checks are also governed by strict rules against coercion, threats and misrepresentation. The fact is card check is a secret ballot. But by conveniently omitting that fact, opponents of EFCA inferred that only the additional secret ballot was "secret." Their crafty rhetoric convinced those not paying close enough attention to side with them and against their own best interests. The plutocrats' goal in this was, obviously, the continuation of their ability to lengthen and hinder the unionization process, which grants them more time to employ other union-busting tactics and spread additional deceptive propaganda. To date, the Employee Free Choice Act has not passed through Congress.

Furthermore, the publicity garnered by the EFCA fight exacerbated anti-union sentiment amongst the general public. By portraying unions as self-interested and un-American, plutocrats convinced the unaware to believe *they* and not the unions were the ones concerned with workers' rights. Give that one the "Judge Judy Test." Which makes the most sense?

Of course, sometimes a union's actions create animosity on their own. When TWU Local 100 last went on a strike, which was illegal but they went anyway in defiance of the law, many New Yorkers were angry at them. Who wants to walk or fight traffic to get to work in the dead of winter? What those New Yorkers should have done was stay home in defiance of the law. The outcomes would have been a much shorter strike and a message sent to plutocrats as to who's the boss!

Some unions have also suffered by being too "successful." There are numerous cases where unions have bargained for, and won, unsustainable pay, benefits and pensions. By not taking the big picture into account, these contracts can, and have, led to forced givebacks and layoffs down the road. It's happened to me, more than once. Additionally, by negotiating financially unfeasible contracts unions can be perceived, and portrayed, as "extortionists."

But it takes two to tango. Reasonably, labor/management negotiations should be just that, a fair give and take from both sides. That, however, requires candor and honesty from both sides. Unfortunately, as former Massachusetts Governor and presidential candidate Mitt Romney said: "corporations are people" – and so are unions. Being people, they have that ingrained prejudice toward their team. I have seen instances where management has caved in to a union just to get them out of their hair. And I have seen instances when that was the case and the union knew it but still agreed to an overly aggressive contract they realized could not be sustained – just to please their team, the membership.

And in fairness, I realize there's good and bad in everything. Sometimes a union's actions attract animosity deservedly. There are many examples of union corruption. But that does not mean it is the norm. Besides being societal organizations, unions are necessarily political organizations – and politics can be dirty – and corrupt.

But to hear it told by certain media and political mouthpieces, funded and influenced by plutocrats, some are led to think all unions are corrupt all the time.

The decline in the favorability and membership of unions is attributable to, like just about everything else is, the exploitation of prejudice through propaganda. And that is accomplished by the clever use of language. Let us examine how.

Infamous events in the state of Wisconsin provide a laboratory for the examination of manipulation through language.

First, let's review the events:

In Wisconsin, in February of 2011, Governor Scott Walker proposed a state budget bill that imposed financial concessions and reductions in collective bargaining rights on public-sector unions. The unions said they would agree to the concessions but not to the reduction of their legal rights. Chaotic protests surrounded the state capitol building for weeks. Democratic members of the State Senate left the chamber in protest, preventing the necessary quorum required for a vote. Republican (Governor Walker's Party) members reframed the bill in order to get it passed without a quorum. Subsequently, a court found the bill violated state law and denied its passage. Finally, the State Supreme Court overturned the lower court's ruling in June of 2011.

Due to the dispute with the unions, proceedings began in November of 2011 to recall Governor Walker. The recall election was held on June 5th of 2012. Despite a disapproval rating of 50-51%, Walker won the election with 53% of the vote. How?

<u>Manipulation through language</u>:

Professor George Lakoff teaches Cognitive Science and Linguistics at UC Berkeley. His associate, Elisabeth Wehling, is a political strategist, and a Linguistics researcher, also at UC Berkeley. Together, they examined how language was used to manipulate the citizens of Wisconsin into voting against their own best interests.

In their article, "The Wisconsin Blues" (*Huffington Post*: June 12, 2012), Lakoff and Wehling explained the logic and reasons that make language manipulation work, using the Wisconsin recall vote as a laboratorial example.

Those of us who Lakoff and Wehling describe as having "mixed values – partly progressive, partly conservative" – whether registered as Democrats, Republicans or Independents (like Bill O'Reilly and me) are the independent thinkers, which would be most of us. And the independent thinkers, who decide according to information as opposed to affiliation, account for the swing vote.

The reason Wisconsinites were convinced to swing the vote against their own best interests was because the dissolute Conservunists in power, and the psychotic plutocrats who control them, bamboozled the sincere conservatives and sincere partly-conservatives to do so. They did this by framing their information to appeal to moral values, which are emotional.

By appealing to policy, which is intellectual, those who truly sought justice for all blew it because, to reiterate what Lakoff and Wehling teach, "morality [emotion] ... trumps policy [intellect]." Of course, we already learned this in our study of "Prejudice: The Main Idea." But it bears repeating, as Lakoff and Wehling also advise, "over and over."

Another example of the above phenomenon, on the national scale, was the re-election of George W. Bush. Since leaving office, Bush has consistently ranked as one of the worst Presidents in history. After his disastrous first term, his re-election was, to many, incomprehensible. But I will never forget the results of an ABC News poll, taken the day after "W's" second election to the White House, which clarified why he won. Participants were asked one question: "Why did you vote for – whoever you voted for?" That was it. Although not asked who they voted for, it was obvious the majority had voted for Bush. And the answer as to why, most often given, was "moral values."

The alarming takeaway from Lakoff and Wehling is that even if we are thinking about what we're thinking, clever appeal to our emotions (propaganda) can override our intellect and make us act against our own best interests. That is why we must be vigilant.

"Perception is reality," goes the slogan. Whoever better uses propaganda to convince more of us that he/she is on our team, be it true or not, wins. What is even more frightening, as was demonstrated by the case of George W. Bush (and repeated in 2016 by Donald Trump), is that actions (apparently) *do not* speak louder than (clever) words.

Remember Ronald Reagan's emotional appeal to the "spiritual and moral values" of a gathering of union members, on Labor Day in 1980, when he (correctly) reminded them; there is no freedom without free unionism?

I have exercised my First Amendment right to disagree with my union when I've felt they were wrong. However, I appreciate the fact that my union, and the American Labor movement in general, has earned all of us freedoms that many people in other parts of this world wish they had. Because of that, Reagan's words resounded with me as well as other partly-conservative-progressives and with partly-progressive-conservatives, too.

Reagan was well schooled in the art of persuasion. He went on to show by his actions that he didn't mean what he said. But what he said (at the time) represented the foundation of our American way of life, i.e., without UNIONISM there is COMMUNISM!

XI

The Good, the Bad and the Ugly

"Beauty is in the eye of the beholder" Margaret Hungerford

Similar to the earlier chapter on "Ideas," in this one, I want to examine several different topics. Much of what follows will be my opinion. By no means do I intend to imply that my opinion ought to be endorsed by anyone else. As I have tried to do on every page of this book, I only present my side as an alternative point of view, which will, hopefully at least, make sense. Toward that effort I will, of course, cite facts, logic and reasons to back up my views. Convincing the reader to agree with me is not the point. Encouraging the reader to consider other points of view is.

On TV, under the title "Pinheads and Patriots," Bill O'Reilly would proclaim his opinion in a memorable way by declaring a person, entity or situation pinheaded or patriotic. I like that format and will now steal it! My segment is called: "The Good, the Bad and the Ugly." As I did with "Ideas," I will simply list my subjects alphabetically.

American Airlines

The Good:

Time for just a little more of my biography: When I got my first airline job, in 1979, it was with TWA. Shortly before they hired me, TWA and the Machinists Union agreed to one of those unsustainable contracts we spoke about in the previous chapter. Basically, everything was downhill from there. Eventually, in 2001, TWA declared bankruptcy, for the third time, and was acquired by American Airlines.

Due to the AA acquisition, I had to move from New York City, the only home I had known since birth, to Kansas City, Missouri and eventually DFW, Texas. But at least I got to keep my decent, well-paying job.

The Bad:

The purchase of TWA was not welcomed by everyone that occupied the upstairs offices at AA. Practicing plutocrat Don Carty was AA's CEO at the time. It was his ultimate decision to make the AA/TWA deal. (That worked out for me. Otherwise, I would have landed on the unemployment line – for the third time – at age 46. Not a good place to be.) Shortly after the merger, due in part to its expense and the 9/11 tragedy, CEO Carty asked the workforce for concessions. That was a first for the AA natives, but we TWA immigrants were used to it. Carty made the case for, and the unions agreed to, rather severe cuts in wages and benefits.

Before the ink was dry on the concessionary contracts, it came to light that Carty had hidden the fact that he and all of AA's senior management were protected from similar concessions. The uproar resulted in Carty's resignation. However, it did not result in any concessions from management.

The Good (again):

After Don Carty was ousted, his underling, Gerard Arpey, became CEO. He brought in a consulting firm that offered to work with the company and the unions in order to improve productivity and, thereby, profits. Everyone agreed that it was worth a try. For a while, things were great! The union workers, the "parasites" who do all the production, shared our expertise with management, the parasitic "producers." All areas and levels of American's operations improved in productivity and profits. AA's stock price soared. CNBC even made a TV special, pointing to American's labor/management "Working Together Plan" as exemplary. The workforce was happy. And we were proud that we were "appreciated" – or so we thought.

The Bad (again):

As it turned out, again, the only appreciation AA management showed was to them selves. As soon as the unions had agreed to help them run the shop, they knew they were looking at a goldmine. So they "awarded" them selves stock-options, which they cashed in at the inflated stock prices that the frontline workers made happen. All we got were promises. But here's the key, none were in writing.

I know what you're thinking: "How could the leadership of *all* the unions have been so stupid?" We "parasites" thought the same thing – three times – because the "producers" awarded them selves stock-options, and us nothing, two more times!

Ultimately, the natives got restless (and so did the immigrants). Moral went down, and brought productivity, profits and the stock price with it. Management's greed killed a Golden Goose. Finally, they needed to find another solution, so they could keep lining their pockets.

The Ugly:

Bankruptcy was "The Final Solution." Gerard Arpey and several other managers, who (like Arpey) at least tried to do the right thing but had their hands tied by the Board of Directors, were pushed out. Arpey was replaced, as CEO, by a cutthroat, plutocrat, with merger experience (AT&T/SBC), named Tom Horton. The next day, AMR Corporation (American Airlines) declared bankruptcy. That was November 29, 2011, five days after Thanksgiving. I was on duty.

While in bankruptcy, US Airways CEO Doug Parker approached the three unions at AA (flight attendants, ground workers and pilots). Parker asked for their support for a merger with AA, giving the impression that he would "take care of us" if we helped him convince AA to make the deal. The unions were overjoyed with their newfound friend and with their astute deal-making, which would save AA again. Of course, I am sure the merger had nothing to do with the fact that Doug Parker and (merger specialist) Tom Horton were old chums who started their careers side-by-side, 25 years earlier, as members of AA's so-called "Brat Pack" of young, whiz-kid managers.

In order for the companies to agree to the "job saving" merger, the unions, of course, had to agree to further concessions and "necessary layoffs." American also offered a buy-out to get rid of as many workers as they could. That's when I made my escape, retiring in 2012.

During bankruptcy proceedings, the court was asked to approve a post-merger severance (golden parachute) for Tom Horton, reported as anywhere between $17 million and $20 million dollars. The judge denied the request, stating it would be "inappropriate" for him to grant it. However, the judge also indicated that once AA emerged from bankruptcy no one could stop it. AA emerged from bankruptcy and the merger with US Airways was finalized on December 9, 2013.

The (somewhat) Good (for some):

After the merger "The New AA's" stock went up again, and the remaining workers were awarded some shares. But those shares came at the cost of concessions added to the pre-bankruptcy concessions that were never repaid – coerced, early retirements – and "job saving" layoffs. (By the way, even some retirees were eligible for stock. I received *two whole shares*, which I was required to pay tax on. But I bought a whole lot more. Like plutocrats, who are crazy but not stupid – I might be stupid, but I'm not crazy!)

I relate the AA saga here not for personal catharsis, but because it contains valuable lessons for us all.

First lesson: GET IT IN WRITING! Even then, thanks to legislation, such as the tax and bankruptcy laws, crafted to enable the "producers" from giving the "parasites" their fair share, we can sometimes lose out. But you can't be blamed for trying, only for not trying. It's a pity that politicians aren't required to put their campaign promises in writing. There's something we should work on!

Second lesson: BE CAREFUL WHAT YOU ASK FOR – as with the "windfall" TWA contract, which led to every subsequent contract being concessionary – OR FORGET TO ASK FOR – as with the unions agreeing to bail out AA without first securing our fair share – YOU MIGHT JUST GET IT!

Third lesson: "GET INVOLVED!" After "you are the union" that is the most often quoted union slogan. To me, it brings to mind the inspiring question: "What can one man do?" With his pamphlet, *Common Sense,* one man, Thomas Paine, inspired our nation to "legitimate revolution."

I got involved in the AA management, stock-option scandal. I wasn't even working as a union representative at the time. I had already gone back to the rank-and-file and was working at my toolbox in an aircraft hangar. But after having been frustrated and insulted by the plutocracy I worked under for so many years, I needed to do something. I decided that my writing skills afforded my best opportunity to make an effort, with an open-letter to the CEO. (See Appendix B for the full letter.)

The letter was published in one, small, local, weekly newspaper, *DFW People*. But that was the best place for it to appear. That newspaper was handed out for free, in large quantities, mainly at DFW Airport, American Airlines' Headquarters. So I knew it would be read by AA management. Additionally, I disseminated my letter by e-mail to as many AA workers as I could. Within the AA system, it went "viral." It was printed out and hung on lockers and bulletin boards at airports from coast to coast. The outcome was a "one time, annual bonus" for the "parasites."

Another instance that outraged me enough to "Get Involved" was the AA bankruptcy. That effort wasn't as successful. It didn't seem to generate as much interest among the workers or the union leadership. Possibly, it was because they were generally too worn down to fight anymore. [O]r the new management was too dissolute to care. Also, *DFW People* had ceased publishing, and a similar newspaper that took its place, *DFW News-Flash*, was apparently not as "progressive." So the article never appeared in any formal publication. Maybe my call-to-arms made the rank-and-file nervous? (See Appendix C for the full article.)

So there you have some examples of what "the great minds" are capable of – betrayal, disloyalty and lack of appreciation – from one man's personal, first hand experience. And the examples of two exercises in protest – one successful and one not – which answer the question: "What can one man do?" The answer is: TRY!

Barack Obama

The Good:

In *Pinheads and Patriots,* Bill O'Reilly said he believed Obama was the most liberal President ever. I have heard O'Reilly also say, on TV, he feels Obama has his heart in the right place. In comparing Bill's two statements, those not thinking about what they're thinking might consider them contradictory. In truth, they demonstrate open-mindedness. And it is only by being open-minded that we, whether progressive or conservative, can "progress."

Remember what my father taught me: "There's good and bad in everything." Although I think Ronald Reagan was a subversive, I liked the fact that he extended Unemployment – at a time when I was unemployed. However, my parents were none too happy with the fact that he, a senior citizen himself, was the first President to deny their Social Security Cost of Living Increase.

Having his heart in the right place, former President Obama consistently tries to do the right thing. But, as I mentioned earlier, while in office, he was constrained by his obligations. The Affordable Care Act, if left alone, would have been beneficial to virtually everyone. Barack Obama's trying was not what hurt many, his ties to his political donors was. As intelligent as he is, I can't think he would have said you could keep your doctor/insurance if you like it had he not believed it. It was the health insurance corporations' tweaking of the law that made a "liar" out of him.

That is the problem with Barack Obama and every other major party politician. They are manipulated by special interests. But it's not their fault, it's ours, because we keep voting for major party politicians.

However, knowing that he could only get elected President by running with a major party, Obama positioned himself to truly make a difference – now that his Presidency has comes to an end.

My belief (and hope) is that, no longer hindered by special interests, citizen Barack Obama will go on to do more good than he could as an elected official.

With his skills as a motivator and organizer, and with President of the United States of America on his resume, Obama could lead the way to breaking down our plutocracy. He might just have what it takes to convince enough of us to stop voting against our own best interests. All he needs to do is stop being so intellectual and become more emotional.

Bill O'Reilly – et al.

The Good:

Well, nobody's perfect! However, irrespective of his personal life, if we are agreed that the job of those who report our information, as described by Professor Brendan Nyhan, is to protect our interests by holding sources accountable and to publically admonish them when they spread misinformation, it is then safe to say nobody does it better than Bill O'Reilly.

As I mentioned in Chapter V, there is a great example in *Pinheads and Patriots*. I would love to describe it here, but I know you will be better served by reading it from the source.

Oh, I've seen other broadcast journalists try it. But almost inevitably, they back off when things get heated. Very few possess O'Reilly's unflappability. The great Mike Wallace was renowned for it. Ted Koppel also comes to mind. And possibly (even before *my* time) Edward R. Murrow. But today, alas, a reporter with true "brass tenacity" is a rarity. In the public interest, it should be a job requirement.

Honorable mention is deserved by CNN's Chris Cuomo. He famously did an interview, a few years back, with Sen. Ted Cruz, where he had the politician cornered – but didn't go far enough. When Cuomo questioned Cruz about his opposition to "Obama-Care," the Senator kept repeating his well-known view that (he thinks) it doesn't work and we should just get rid of it. Cuomo kept the pressure on by asking Cruz if he thought he was responsible, as a Senator, to then find a solution. That's when Cruz sarcastically accused Cuomo of trying to "lecture" him.

Cuomo definitely showed he's got what it takes to do the job. However, although he does his homework and sticks to his guns, he seems to have the need to maintain polite decorum. What I would have liked to see Cuomo do (figuratively) was grab Cruz by the lapels when he gave him the chance.

When Cruz accused Cuomo of "lecturing" him, it would have been nice to hear Cuomo say: Hold on! I said you're a Senator. I said your job is to find solutions. Both are true statements. If you consider that a lecture, then you're a thin-skinned crybaby and obviously not qualified to be a Senator!

But Cuomo kept the heat on, albeit politely. When he finally cornered Cruz by asking what his alternative was Cruz's answer was that we should allow "competition." At that point they were running out of time and, having at least gotten "an answer," Cuomo brought the interview to a close.

Since everyone already knows that Cruz is a Laissez-faire advocate, here was another chance to hold him up to *the mirror of truth:* So Senator, you are essentially saying we ought to go back to the previous system, where lack of regulation allowed health insurance corporations to do everything you criticize "Obama-Care" for. The only difference being, they should be able to do it without accountability!

Cuomo has potential. But he makes the mistake that most reasonable people make, which was revealed to us by Professors Lakoff and Wehling. He insists on being, well, reasonable as opposed to getting emotional.

Bill O'Reilly, on the other hand, although reasonable, has no problem getting emotional – or even unreasonable – when dealing with an unreasonable jerk.

Congress

(As intended) The Good:

Again, I turn to Patrick J. Buchanan, who described the intent of the Constitution regarding the duties of the Congress in *Where the Right Went Wrong:*

The first article of the Constitution outlines the framework and authority of the Legislature (The Congress). Congress shall be the one and only initiator of all laws (excepting the Constitution's actual clauses). Only Congress shall approve the acquiring and/or disbursement of funds. Congress shall be responsible for supporting, regulating and governing the Military, and for declarations of war. Except for the mere presence of the Supreme Court, Congress shall institute and administrate the judiciary system. Congress shall have the power of impeachment over all executive and judiciary branch members. However, Congress members shall be accountable (only) to the Congress itself for their personal, official behavior.

(As is) The Bad:

Shall we examine the duties of the Congress, as described above, how it has shirked its duties, and why?

Article one of the U.S. Constitution dictates that Congress shall be the one and only initiator of all laws. Article three establishes the Judiciary (Supreme Court) with authorization for interpretation and application of laws to particular cases. It does not authorize the Supreme Court to be the initiator of laws.

Congress, however, has increasingly relinquished its power as the initiator of laws to the Supreme Court. One example was Roe v Wade, in which the Supreme Court *legalized* abortion. Whether one agrees with the decision or not, the point is it wasn't their job – it was the job of the Congress.

The disputed Presidential election of 2000 resulted in the Bush v Gore decision by the Supreme Court, overruling the decision of the Florida State Supreme Court, the state in which the decision was necessary. In a prior, contested presidential election (1876) Congress established the Electoral Commission Act – a law – creating a body to resolve the dispute. As it turned out, the Commission was split along Party lines and its decision was as controversial as the Bush v Gore decision. But again, the point is, establishing the legality of the election was not the job of the Supreme Court – it was the job of the Congress.

Article one of the U.S. Constitution dictates that only Congress shall approve the acquiring and/or disbursement of funds. In 1913, the Federal Reserve was created. Thereby, the Congress abdicated its duty to protect the United States economy. Since then the "Fed," not our elected representatives, has controlled the nation's treasure.

Article one of the U.S. Constitution dictates that Congress shall be responsible for supporting, regulating and governing the Military, and for declarations of war. Yet, Korea, Vietnam and Serbia are all examples of acts of war that were initiated without declarations from the Congress. In still another instance, when they did fulfill their responsibility, the Congress was heavily criticized for not considering all relevant factors thoroughly enough. When President George W. Bush asked the Congress to declare war on Iraq, they capitulated. They did so despite the facts that Iraq had not attacked or even threatened to attack the United States. Furthermore, Iraq allowed U.N. inspectors, as requested, to search for the existence of so-called "weapons of mass destruction" (Bush's main rationale in wanting to go to war). Additionally, none of these weapons were, or ever have been, found.

Finally, Article one of the U.S. Constitution dictates that except for the mere presence of the Supreme Court, Congress shall institute and administrate the judiciary system. Congress shall have the power of impeachment over all executive and judiciary branch members. However, Congress members shall be accountable (only) to the Congress itself for their personal, official behavior.

Since the founding of the United States of America, the Congress has only impeached three members of the Executive Branch of the Federal Government. They were: President Andrew Johnson, for firing a member of "his" cabinet that the Congress favored, and President William J. Clinton, for lying about cheating on his wife. Both were acquitted. The third was Secretary of War (1869-1876) William Belknap, for accepting bribes. Belknap was also acquitted, after resigning.

Only one member of the Judicial Branch has ever been impeached, Supreme Court Justice Samuel Chase, because he disagreed with President Thomas Jefferson's politics. Chase was also acquitted. Additionally, Supreme Court Justices have lifetime tenure. Even if they become incapacitated, or cannot perform their function for any other reason, no means exist to effect their removal.

There are numerous examples of failure by the Congress to carry out the duties they are charged with in the Constitution. And although Congress members shall be accountable (only) to the Congress itself for their personal, official behavior, self-serving members, like Senator Ted Cruz and others who are only interested in pleasing those able to vote for them, aren't held accountable for their behavior. Why is the Congress, as a body, failing in its job so miserably? Because (they believe) it's in their best interests.

Once again, Pat Buchanan explained the logic behind that mindset, in his book:

What motivates the Congress to surrender its authority to Presidents, Justices, and other officials? The nasty truth is that Congress members do not want to be held accountable for using their authority. They no longer wish to govern. Democrats and Republicans want to legislate (only) issues their constituencies will approve, and reward with votes – but let others make decisions that might be unpopular.

Congress members would rather give the impression of power than incur the risk of the responsibility of power. An incorrect vote might cost them their [cushy] jobs. Finally, Buchanan described what's in it for the Conservunists: The neo-cons are only interested in presidential supremacy and interventionism. They are intolerant of regulations and constraints, including those cited in the Constitution, which might restrict the President's ability to wage war.

All this begs we ask the question: "How can we fix this?" Evidently, since the Democratic and Republican Parties are now *hardly dissimilar*, and the types that should be "run out of town," the obvious answer is RUN THEM OUT OF TOWN!

Stop voting for Democratic or Republican *politicians* and start voting for Independent *representatives* and keep repeating that "over and over"!

Demagogues

The Good:

Believe it or not, at one time demagoguery was not considered to be something negative. According to the *Oxford English Dictionary* the word demagogue originated in ancient Greece and Rome, and simply meant: "a leader or orator who espoused the cause of the common people."

The Bad:

It didn't take long for some of those leaders to realize they could use their oratory skills to convince the common people to espouse *their* causes. Again according to *Oxford*, demagogue now means: "a political leader who seeks support by appealing to popular desires and prejudices rather than by using rational argument."

Professor of Rhetoric and Writing at the University of Texas at Austin, Patricia Roberts-Miller wrote an essay titled "Characteristics of Demagoguery." (It can be found on the university's website, or just *Google* the title, "Characteristics of Demagoguery.")

In her paper, Professor Roberts-Miller explains how demagogues convince themselves they are right and righteous, and convince others to act against their own best interests, by targeting "the main idea" (of Chapter VI) "Prejudice."

She defines Demagoguery as ... a dialogue promising security and relief from the burden of discourse by describing civic guidelines as how much and in what ways [but not "if"] outgroups must be penalized because of the ingroup's troubles. (In other words, it's always someone else's fault.)

Demagoguery is invariably divisive ... but can be made to appear reasonable by the use of statistics, figures, and allegations, as well as analytics. (See: "The Expert Fallacy" in Chapter VII.)

Professor Roberts-Miller describes "naive realism," a characteristic of demagoguery, which ... allows uncomplicated descriptions [because they are more likely to relate to perceptions], and encourages "confirmation bias" [since perceptions come faster and more readily when descriptions confirm beliefs]. (See: "The Phenomenon of Backfire" in Chapter V, particularly the caveat from Professor Brendan Nyhan, "it's absolutely threatening to admit you're wrong.")

She points out the danger in this type of thinking: ... perplexingly, believing oneself able to unfailingly see things precisely as they are makes one more likely to be not only incorrect – but incorrect in the identical manner and about the identical matters – again and again. (Remember what Confucius said: "Real knowledge is to know the extent of one's ignorance.")

She advises that … authoritarianism greatly corresponds to demagoguery. "Authoritarian submission" is the eagerness to obey authority and place tight restrictions on criticism of authority figures. Next, authoritarians promote restrictions for those they perceive as harmful to authority. "Authoritarian aggression" is strengthened by the belief that it is approved by, and protects, confirmed authority. Therefore, theoretically, authoritarianism is intimately correspondent to "social dominance." Lastly, authoritarians tend to follow traditions that society and its authorities espouse. Authoritarian aggressiveness often targets those considered unorthodox or aberrant, like gays. (See: "Fear of The Other": Also see: Chapter VI for Adorno's views on how an authoritarian personality leads to prejudice.) And she adds: Authoritarians are afraid of change, but surprisingly, will welcome extreme changes if defined as reinforcement or restoration of values considered to be long-established and/or normal. (See: In Chapter I, the definition of "Conservative.")

In her discussion about "Identity as logic," Professor Roberts-Miller precisely describes the attitudes of Ayn Rand's true believers: Demagoguery's principal assumption, and most alluring promise, is the secure classification of identity. This classification is a pecking order, too, wherein certain persons deserve more because they are better – because of their identity – no matter how they behave. This creates a paradox where the ingroup [being "better"] enjoys a curtailed code of ethics, allowing them to act badly. An outcome is; the equivalent conduct is described positively for the ingroup [hard working] but negatively for the outgroup [greedy]. This difference allows for "projection."

She defined projection: Demagoguery depends upon denunciation of the outgroup for the behavior of the ingroup. This stance is required for "scapegoating" [blaming an *other* for the ingroup's troubles]. Projection has various types. (For our purposes we only need to examine one.)

"Cunning projection" ... creates distraction in bystanders, and makes it difficult for them to comprehend circumstances. ... making it necessary for bystanders to research the circumstances ... Most often, bystanders will not bother, and will base their decision on who they find more "likeable." ... This tactic works exceptionally well with those who think a person's beliefs can be known from the values they profess, and those who believe another's behavior can be predicted from how they speak about values [... those who say the "right" things – don't do wrong things].

(What the professor sheds light on here is the truth that a con-artist cannot be effective unless "likeable" and how he/she achieves that persona. First: By complicating an issue for bystanders, those being the independent thinkers or swing voters, demagogues necessitate further research. Demagogues know, from studying the psychology of persuasion, most bystanders won't be troubled with thinking about what they're thinking [researching] and their brains will seek a shortcut. Second: They create the shortcut by using language that makes them appear to belong to the bystanders' team. Examples: (1) The Wisconsin plutocracy convincing the most bystanders to keep them in power by portraying themselves as "hard-working" and hard-working people as "greedy." (2) Although having already proven he was feckless, George W. Bush getting re-elected by claiming to share "moral values" with the most bystanders.)

"Victimization" is still another characteristic of demagoguery. Professor Roberts-Miller explains the mentality: The ingroup feels, and portrays itself as, victimized by the same circumstances and treatment encountered by the outgroup, which is a sort of "political narcissism." (See: In Chapter VIII, the philosophy of Ayn Rand. Consider: The claims of the so-called "One Percent" that they should not have to pay taxes equal to the "Ninety-Nine Percent" because they "work harder." Also, I think, the mentality of "victimization" can be explained much more simply and descriptively: Being a selfish crybaby!)

Finally, the professor discussed the use of "metaphors" in demagoguery. Metaphors are used to make the ingroup look good with terms such as: Moral, pure, self-controlled and strong. And the outgroup look bad with: Immoral, indecent, unrestrained and weak. (Have you noticed a pattern with those metaphors? The good ones are relentlessly used to describe the Right, and the bad ones; the Left. Why would that be? Most likely because, as Pat Buchanan demonstrated, the Conservative Right has been hijacked by Conservunist plutocrats.)

The Ugly:

Let us now look at just a few beloved demagogues, and I don't mean that sarcastically. Remember, if they weren't "likeable" demagogues could not be successful. There are certainly many, probably some on radio I haven't even heard of. But here I will just work on those who seem to be the most popular (likeable) and, therefore, the most dangerous.

Ann Coulter:

(I put her first only because her name starts with "A." And I will admit I'm trying very hard to rein-in the sarcasm. That's because – although she and the others I will discuss are all easy targets for comedy – they are also dangerous, subversive, unpatriotic, plutocrat-puppets. As such, I want to expose them to *the mirror of truth* with facts, logic and reason. Oh, I promise to ridicule them at every opportunity, but only when the opportunity is justified. That is because "justified ridicule" is a powerful weapon for exposing injustice. An example being my open letter to the CEO of American Airlines [see: Appendix B]. Anyway – back to "Tokyo Rose.")

Ann Coulter's contribution to the world can be summed up in one word: Pornography. Nearly everything she spits out, either orally or in print, can be defined as "... utterly without redeeming social value," i.e., "obscenity." In her case, the obscenity is in the form of "hate speech" that "... will lead to imminent hate violence." Although, according to the Supreme Court, such speech is protected by the First Amendment. But that does not make it any less obscene. Coulter, ironically, declares she is not a "fan" of the First Amendment. (Although it allows her to make a nice living as a "pornographer.")

In an interview with *The Telegraph* (July 19, 2002), Coulter praised Mao Tse-tung's logic that it's good to be assaulted by one's enemies, adding that the more violent they are the more satisfied she is.

In *The Guardian* (May 16, 2003), she mentioned her father (a lawyer), praising him for being a "union buster."

From the *Washington Post* (August 1, 2000), she likes Bush because she believes he hates liberals.

From FNC (October 6, 2004), the best way to talk to liberals is with a "baseball bat."

From *Politically Incorrect* (December18, 1997), school children should be taught to use guns instead of pray.

From *The Observer* (August 25, 2002), she was disappointed Timothy McVeigh didn't choose the New York Times building. In a later interview (June 26, 2003) she was asked if she regretted saying that: Yes, she said, adding that he should have waited until only the editors and reporters were left in the building.

June 2009: I wouldn't personally murder an abortionist, but I don't wish to force my principles on anyone else.

January 26, 2006: She commented in a speech that someone should poison Supreme Court Justice John Paul Stevens. Then she added, "for the media" that she was just joking.

October 2007: She claimed that Jews should be "perfected." That is, become Christians.

Coulter titled one of her books (appealingly) *If Democrats Had Any Brains, They'd Be Republicans*. In it she wrote about how she can, proudly, sink lower every time they think she can't. Remarking that if Hitler were alive today, Republicans would recommend he condemn her and progressives would say that he may have killed millions but he hates Ann Coulter, so he must be OK.

Let us recap: Coulter proclaims herself a patriotic American and staunch anti-Communist. But she likes to quote Chairman Mao and is *satisfied* when she can make other Americans violent. She often talks about Ronald Reagan as if he should be sainted and is proud her father was a "union buster." This simply demonstrates Conservunist hypocrisy. Reagan, as we know, was also a Conservunist hypocrite. On the one hand, he proclaimed himself a patriotic, anti-Communist, American – and spoke about how unionism protected and preserved not only our spiritual and moral values but our freedom as well. On the other hand, President of the United States, defender of the Constitution, as well as former union president, Reagan worked tirelessly to break unions and turn America into a quasi-Communist, degenerated workers' state. It's also likely that Coulter's, conservative father, as well as she and the rest of her family, is a Republican. The odds are pretty high that he reveres Reagan as much as his daughter. And according to the teachings of Professor of Cognitive Science George Lakoff, the odds are also pretty high that Coulter's dad's conservative, moral values make him a strict authoritarian, who ultimately determines good and bad, and disciplines with punishment. The strict father mentality of conservatives is why they gravitate toward candidates like Reagan, and Donald Trump, who tell them they will *take care of everything.*

Coulter announces that she likes someone because she believes he hates those who disagree with her. She advises that a baseball bat be used as a strategy of debate. While considering herself a "perfect" Christian, she teaches that school children should carry guns instead of pray – journalists she disagrees with, abortion doctors and a Supreme Court Justice should be killed – and Jews (because they aren't Christians) need to be "perfected."

Although she fondly recalls her privileged, conservative upbringing, Coulter boasts about how far she can sink. She jokes that she ought to be thought of as lower than Hitler and that Republicans, her team, would support the leader of the Nazi Party.

It's apparent that Coulter is even crazier than the psychotic plutocrats she serves and worships. However, like them, she isn't stupid. Consider something else she said, and as you do, remember the lessons we have already learned:

Propaganda is effective because most people are too busy and/or stupid to see it. People think they comprehend bias and recognize it, which is ridiculous. They surely don't. (FOX News, October 6, 2004)

You might think it stupid for Coulter, her vocation being "demagogue," to publicly say that. And even refer to her audience as stupid. It would be if it were not true. The fact is – she happens to be right. And we already know why from the little bit we have learned about how our brains, prejudice and propaganda work. Please re-read Coulter's statement about why propaganda is effective. Now consider the following summarization: Propaganda is effective ON ANYONE because they don't THINK ABOUT WHAT THEY'RE THINKING!

Coulter's popularity, despite her behavior, is further evidence that her observation about propaganda is correct. It also shows that being popular overrides being a menace to society. Although her book titles and opinions are purposely insulting, not only to her adversaries but also to her admirers – her remarks are laced with bigotry and calls for violence – and she brazenly refers to her own audience as stupid – the astonishing fact is Coulter still has an audience! The more disappointing aspect is she continues to reach an audience through appearances on (supposedly) unbiased outlets. The "mainstream media," which she ridicules, continues to allow her a forum. As far as I am aware, this courtesy is not afforded to any other pornographer.

To punctuate this examination, I call on someone with a lot more experience in the art of persuasion than I, Bill O'Reilly, from the book *Soulless: Ann Coulter and the Right-Wing Church of Hate*, by Susan Estrich: If Coulter wants to convince people to embrace her point-of-view, her personal attacks are foolish …. They hurt, rather than help, conservatives, since they strengthen the opposition's opinions; conservatives are mean-spirited, lack self-control, etc. Thank you, Mr. O'Reilly!

Glenn Beck:

Since leaving FNC, Glenn Beck seems to have toned down his act. But that might only appear so, due to his no longer having regular exposure to vast multitudes via television. However, an examination of his recorded work reveals some of the ugliest of demagoguery.

Beck's *shtick* is a classic example of "The Expert Fallacy." With his blackboards and books, he presents himself as some kind of scholar. He favors bowties and sweaters, to appear as a father figure. And with his propensity for shedding tears on cue, he entices his audience to believe he feels their pain.

Undoubtedly, Beck's most effective tools are his pleas to "don't take my word for it," "have an open mind" and especially "do your own homework." Thus, he gains trust by implying that he welcomes fact-checking. But, as a well-schooled propagandist, he knows his audience will take his word and will not have open minds or do their homework. That is why they are his audience. They want to be fed their information by their favorite "expert." Beck is highly aware of the fact that his demagoguery works because his devotees are, as his comrade Coulter cites, too busy and/or stupid to see it.

In preparing this report on Glenn Beck, I did *my* homework. And I strongly recommend that anyone who cares about not being duped into acting against their own best interests do likewise. Every examination I did revealed examples of multiple propaganda methods, including: Ad hominem, Ad nauseam, Appeal to fear and Appeal to prejudice, Disinformation, Labeling and/or Name-calling, Flag Waving and Lying and Deception.

One of Beck's favorite devices is to take facts or quotes out of context and twist them into meaning what he would like them to mean. Otherwise, he'll dispense with the obfuscation entirely and just claim something or someone is what he wants to portray them as, without any proof whatsoever.

Let us look at just one case as an example of Beck's blatant distortions.

YouTube has countless videos of Beck's ramblings. I picked one, listened to what Beck had to say (with an open mind) and then checked the facts. The one I watched was called: "Howard Zinn's A People's History of the United States Glenn Beck breaks down the Propaganda."

Before seeing the Beck video, I had no idea who Howard Zinn was. Glenn Beck tells us Zinn was (he died in 2010) a "Communist activist." Beck also said (actor) Matt Damon was Zinn's neighbor as a child (which is true) and because he was "mentored" by Zinn, Damon is a "radical Leftist." Beck played an out-take from an interview Zinn did, where Zinn said he wanted to be remembered for presenting a new school of thought about war, equality, and human rights. Beck stopped the tape there and declared that Zinn's new school of thought was "Communism" and making America look like an evil oppressor in the world. Then, I did my homework.

The very easy-to-find truth (if one wants to find it) is that Howard Zinn was a Professor of Political Science and History, as well as an author, playwright and social activist.

Zinn also enlisted to fight the Nazis during World War II. He served in the United States Army Air Force as a bombardier. In that role, he learned, he had been made to participate in a bombing raid in which he dropped napalm on a French resort village, which killed over one thousand Allied civilians. (Zinn recounts this episode in his book *The Politics of History*.) That experience and others involving indiscriminate, needless killing helped provoke Zinn's espousing of social activism and especially his anti-war stance.

While teaching at Spelman College in Atlanta, Georgia, from 1956 to 1963, Professor Zinn became active in the civil rights movement. At the time, Zinn wrote about seeing flagrant violations of the Bill of Rights, and of how Federal law enforcement stood by as civil rights workers were attacked by racists. ("Finishing School for Pickets" By Howard Zinn: *The Nation*, August 6, 1960) Finally, he was let go by Spelman, for aligning himself with his students in the fight for civil rights, even though his position was tenured.

So far we have learned Howard Zinn was an educator, artist and social activist. He was also, one can argue, a war hero, not because he fought to defend his country in a war, but because he fought against indiscriminate and unnecessary war. And he was willing to lose his job in order to defend the Constitution of the United States of America, in defiance of his government, when he observed they were unwilling. All of which are admirable pursuits of moral value.

Glenn Beck can also be classified as a social activist. However, when the activities of another do not reflect his own "moral values," rather than explain why, he simply labels them a Communist. In the case of Howard Zinn, let us see where Beck came up with that tidbit of Ad hominem, Disinformation.

In 1949, the FBI began investigating Howard Zinn for association with what they "considered" Communist front groups and because "informants" told the Bureau he was a member of the Communist Party of the United States of America (CPUSA). Zinn denied being a Communist. However, he added that he was involved with certain groups which might be thought of as Communist fronts because he believed we had a right to think what we want. (He probably thought so because of that pesky United States Constitution.) (Information contained in FBI file on Howard Zinn: Released in 2010 by Freedom of Information Act [FOIA] request)

In the 1960's, Zinn was again hounded by the FBI because of his opposition to the Vietnam War, association with Dr. Martin Luther King, Jr. and for exposing the FBI's declining to intervene against racist mob attacks on civil rights workers.

(Information contained in FBI file on Howard Zinn: Released in 2010 by Freedom of Information Act [FOIA] request)

Remember, this happened at a time when megalomaniac J. Edgar Hoover (who *was* the FBI) and demagogue Senator Joe McCarthy both, like Glenn Beck, regularly denounced anyone they cared to as "Communists," just to further their careers simply because they could.

Now, let's give the professor the opportunity Glenn Beck would not. Beck claimed that Zinn's new school of thought was "Communism" and making America look like an evil oppressor in the world. He did so after showing a short out-take. Rather than taking Glenn Beck's word, let us hear what that new school of thought was from the man who did the thinking and draw our own conclusion.

Howard Zinn wrote a letter to the *New York Times* in 2007, discussing his work. In it he cited that his history chronicled those who struggled against human rights violations, such as Frederick Douglass, William Lloyd Garrison, Fannie Lou Hamer, and Bob Moses. He spoke of organizers in the Labor movement, like Big Bill Haywood, Mother Jones, and César Chávez, who fought for workers' rights. He explained the socialists and others who led protests against militarism and war: Eugene V. Debs, Helen Keller, the Rev. Daniel Berrigan, Cindy Sheehan. He described his heroes as not being those like Theodore Roosevelt, who praised one of his generals for a Filipino massacre, but Mark Twain, who condemned it and ridiculed imperialism.

In his letter, Professor Zinn said he wanted the young to realize America is a great country that has been overtaken by those who disregard human rights and constitutional freedoms. Americans are compassionate and good. The Declaration of Independence, which states our equal rights to "life, liberty, and the pursuit of happiness," expresses our paramount values. In my book, Zinn said, I point out that our history is a struggle against dishonest plutocrats and warmongers; a struggle to make those values real – and we all, no matter what our age, can find pride by joining in that.

So if we want to take Glenn Beck's word, from his short out-take, (then) are we to believe Professor Zinn was a "Communist" because he taught the history (which is all true): Of great and brave Americans who fought slavery instead of those who owned slaves? Of Americans who risked their lives so you and I could have fairness in the workplace instead of those who exploited their fellow Americans? And of Americans with the courage to speak out against war for profit and the needless waste of lives instead of those who profited from war?

Was Howard Zinn a "Communist" because he taught that American ideals, as expressed in our Declaration of Independence, are to be defended against self-interested subversives who would gladly destroy America for their own profit?

Or is it more likely that Glenn Beck is a subversive, in the employ of subversives, and attacks people like Howard Zinn in order to glorify himself and his subversive comrades?

Another writer, Bob Herbert, discussed Zinn's teachings, also in the *New York Times*, in 2010. Mr. Herbert wrote that Zinn was denounced for pulling back the curtain on American history and exposing the gory details that hide there. Was Zinn radical for asserting that workers ought to be treated fairly – or corporations are too powerful over us and our Government – or we need to find alternatives to the horrors of war – or that minorities and whites are entitled to equal rights – or that elites in business and government don't share the same interests as those of us who must struggle, day to day, to simply survive?

Indeed, what was radical about that? The only evident answer is that a lot of it cuts into the profits of plutocrat subversives.

Speaking in 2009, Howard Zinn candidly described himself as a bit of a socialist, which, by the way, is not a crime in America. For that matter, neither is being a Communist. He went on to discuss how the philosophy of socialism was once popular in America and how it came to be vilified because of its exploitation and misrepresentation by Soviet Communists:

Let's discuss socialism. At the turn of the [last] century, socialism got a bad name because of the Soviet Union. Before that, in America, it had a good name. I believe it's vital that socialism return to our country's discussion. It had the likes of Eugene Debs, Clarence Darrow, Mother Jones, and Emma Goldman. Several million people were reading socialist newspapers. Socialism taught that society can be gentler and kinder – and that we should share – and that capitalism should produce what we need, not just what is profitable. The word "socialism" should not be shied away from, we need to exceed capitalism.

WOW! Helen Keller? Clarence Darrow? Mother Jones? Kinder, gentler society? Share? Exceed capitalism? That's Communism? I suppose it is to a Conservunist, Atlas-Masturbator who doesn't care about kindness, improving society, sharing, or making capitalism "better."

Since Glenn Beck also slandered Matt Damon in the same show, by declaring him a "radical Leftist," let's check that out as well. Here are some facts about the actor, Matt Damon, which are very easy to look up:

Matt Damon's father is a stockbroker (Obviously, Matt did not inherit his "radicalism."). His mother is a university professor (Oh? Then again?).

Matt Damon works with and donates to charities involved in getting clean water to parts of the world where it is scarce, preventing mass atrocities, fighting AIDS, poverty and hunger in the United States and elsewhere, among other humanitarian efforts.

Matt Damon supports the Democratic Party. He has been critical of Republicans as well as Democrats and the American political system in general.

Nothing seems apparently "radical" or "Leftist"? Except, maybe that part about being critical of *Republicans* as well as Democrats?

Getting back to Glenn Beck's main focus, Howard Zinn, in this examination of demagoguery, the best person to sum it up is Zinn himself.

Forty-one years after Spelman College in Atlanta fired Professor Zinn, they invited him back, in 2005. He was asked to deliver the commencement address to the graduating class and received an honorary Doctorate in Humane Letters.

Zinn titled the commencement speech he gave "Against Discouragement." Part of what he talked about was how we must not give in to discouragement. We can make change if we are justified and persistent. TV, newspapers, and the government might attempt to fool us, but truth will always come out. Truth is more powerful than lies.

However, never forget, truth will only come out if we look for it. Accepting claims without verifying them even if (maybe especially if [?]) we are told "don't take my word for it" is, in itself, acting against our own best interests.

Another Yiddish word comes to mind that sums up the *shtick* of Glenn Beck. It even rhymes with Beck: *DRECK*. (Look it up. Don't take my word for it.)

Rush Limbaugh:

Limbaugh is the darling of the Right Wing. He is the highest paid and highest rated (most successful) demagogue in the history of broadcasting. He has won broadcasting awards for the level of success he has achieved in the field, and awards from conservative groups for the level of success he has achieved in preaching their gospel.

From all of the above-mentioned success, Rush Limbaugh easily earns the crown of "Duke of Demagogues." All that success also makes him one of America's most dangerous subversives. However, what he preaches seems to make all that success defy all logic and reason. But does it, really?

You might recall that in April of 2014, one, Mr. Donald Sterling, owner of the Los Angeles Clippers professional basketball team, was fined $2.5 million, forced to sell the team and banned from the NBA for life, because of racial slurs he made in private, which became public knowledge.

However, Rush Limbaugh has openly made public, racial slurs in his broadcasts. Example: He once told a black caller to his radio program (who he had trouble understanding) to call him back after he took the bone out of his nose. (*Newsday*: October 8, 1990) And he's still on the air.

Limbaugh has also made blanket, derogatory, sexist remarks toward women. Example: Feminism started so ugly women can more easily become a part of society. (*Time* magazine: October 26, 1992) In his book *The Way Things Ought to Be* from 1992 (page 193), he referred to feminists as "feminazis." (Although, he gave a friend of his "credit" for coining the term.) And he's still on the air.

On January 16, 2009, referring to the, soon to begin, Obama Presidency, Limbaugh said he hoped Obama failed. Later that year, on March 4, Rush told the *Washington Post* he wanted to see Obama's policies fail, not the man himself. (That's even worse! If you want to see any President's policies fail you want to see America fail. But remember who Rush Limbaugh's, and all Conservunist's, "patron saint" is, Ronald Reagan, who said "… government is the problem." Their goal is to abolish the government, so their plutocrat providers can enslave the rest of us.) And he's still on the air.

In October of 2006, Rush accused (actor) Michael J. Fox, who has Parkinson's disease, of hamming-up his affliction in a PSA (public service announcement) the actor did for the funding of stem cell research. He even mimicked Fox's shaking. And he's still on the air.

In 2012, law student Sandra Fluke spoke before The House Democratic Steering and Policy Committee to provide evidence that contraceptives should be covered by health insurance. Not only for birth control but also because contraceptive hormones are necessary in the treatment of certain diseases. Limbaugh called her a "slut" and "prostitute" on the air. Rush's remarks were condemned by those on the Right as well as Left. Moreover, he lost several of his program sponsors. The backlash caused Limbaugh to give Ms. Fluke an apology, which was, however, categorized as insincere by those on the Right as well as Left. And he's still on the air.

In 2013, after Pope Francis called on global leaders to combat inequality and poverty Rush Limbaugh called the Pope's comments "Marxism." And he's still, well, you know.

The utterances that Rush Limbaugh has gotten away with and survived are, in a word, ASTOUNDING.

There was a time, not too long ago, when any broadcaster who made fun of someone's race, equated women to Nazis, said he hoped the President failed, ridiculed a person's disability, slandered someone, or effectively called the Pope a Commie, would never be heard from again. However, today that has all changed. And guess who changed it? Ronald Reagan.

In 1949, the Federal Communications Commission (FCC) enacted the "Fairness Doctrine," which required that broadcasters allow opposing views on matters of public interest (when) considered controversial. In 1987 the FCC, which at the time was Chaired by (Reagan appointee) Dennis R. Patrick, voted to abrogate the Fairness Doctrine. Two months prior to the FCC vote, Congress tried to enact legislation that would modify the Fairness Doctrine, in an attempt to prevent its outright repeal. Reagan vetoed it.

Ever since the abolition of the Fairness Doctrine we have seen the proliferation of programs and entire networks, such as FNC and MSNBC, which only present their personal, editorial slant. And they are no longer required to allow opposing views.

Furthermore, demagogue broadcasters like Rush Limbaugh push the envelope of propaganda to see how much of their un-fairness doctrine they can spread. In 2005, Wall Street Journal editor Daniel Henninger wrote: "Ronald Reagan tore down this wall [the Fairness Doctrine] in 1987 ... and Rush Limbaugh was the first man to proclaim himself liberated from the East Germany of liberal media domination."

On the day broadcasting icon Barbara Walters retired, she appeared on *The O'Reilly Factor*. At one point in their conversation/interview, Bill commented on how he thought journalism, in America, has become different, especially on TV, adding that he now sees it as a means of promoting personal "agendas." O'Reilly hit the nail on the head. NOW - he, and you, knows WHY he has observed this change!

But Rush Limbaugh's success is attributable to forces much deeper and more complicated than loose laws that allow loose lips.

Let us ask our selves: Why was Donald Sterling fined $2.5 million, forced to sell his team and banned from the league for life, because he made a racial slur - but - Rush Limbaugh gets away with it, as well as countless other examples of ad-hominem, slander? If we have learned anything from the previous pages, we know the answer is MONEY. Mr. Sterling's enterprise, the L.A. Clippers, generated money for him. Mr. Limbaugh's enterprise, his broadcasts, generates money for his employers, namely, plutocrats who protect him because they want him to keep doing exactly what he is doing. That is, to convince otherwise innocent, good-hearted Americans they are better than, and should be in fear of, *the other*.

After loose laws and MONEY, the third force at work in Rush Limbaugh's success formula is the fact that he's acutely aware of just who his audience is and knows how much they will let him get away with, as long as he does it in such a way that keeps them believing he is one of their team.

A Pew Research Center profile (September 2012) indicated that Rush Limbaugh's audience is made up of those: Mostly over the age of 50 (set in their ways), mostly men (father figures), mostly conservatives (authoritarian personalities) and most of those are Republicans.

But the most revealing demographic was this: A whopping 77% of Limbaugh's audience said they "trust a few sources more than others." In other words, they only want to hear what they want to hear, so they don't have to THINK ABOUT WHAT THEY'RE THINKING!

I know a few Limbaugh lovers personally. As the "baby" of my generation (at age 63), all of my first cousins are in their eighties and nineties. And the older ones helped to save the world, because they all fought in World War II. I love, or more accurately, I *revere* these guys. I would jump in front of a bullet for any one of them. That is why it pains me so much to see them bamboozled by Limbaugh's bloviating. But I realize that Rush knows how to push their buttons.

Because of their age they are set in their ways. Because they are all fathers, and conservatives, they have authoritarian personalities. And they, pretty much, distrust anyone who is not on their "team." They tease me for being a LIBERAL and I let them. I don't argue politics with them because their wives are all great cooks and I don't want to spoil dinner. All I will say to them is what I have repeatedly said in this book: "We need to stop voting for politicians of either major party because they are beholden to the plutocrats who buy their allegiance – not US!" That always makes them get quiet, look me in the eye, and begin nodding in agreement.

However, I know that come Election Day they will do what they have always done because they are set in their ways. And I realize they believe Rush Limbaugh when he tells them to be distrustful of those Liberals, Marxists, "feminazis," the "wrong" President, promiscuous "sluts," "ham" actors and, of course, people from "inferior" races. That's because, what Limbaugh is saying to them is: You are *right* and if you do as I say you will preserve your *authority!*

Sean Hannity – et al.:

The biggest boon to Hannity's career at FNC was Bill O'Reilly getting the bum's rush. At least O'Reilly would entertain opposing viewpoints. Occasionally, he might even admit he was wrong. Bill O'Reilly was also respected (professionally) by highly-regarded colleagues, such as Barbara Walters and Ted Koppel. O'Reilly's presence in the network's lineup seemed to have a tempering effect on Hannity's and others' outrageous outrage.

Now that O'Reilly is out at FNC and Trump is in the White House, the commentators (not the reporters), especially Hannity, have no interest in the truth but only in their side. Prime-time at FOX has become a relentless barrage of <u>sophistry</u>; argument that is seemingly plausible though actually invalid and misleading. (*Dictionary.com*)

When a crazed man shot at Republican, Congress members while they practiced for a baseball game, I intentionally watched FNC. The reporting was just as accurate and factual as it was on every other news outlet. But the FOX commentators, especially Sean Hannity, had no use for facts.

This was a chance to admit how the hate speech, we are constantly bombarded with, sets off maniacs like the guy with a gun at the ball field. This was a time to bring Congress members from both sides together, like they did themselves, to demonstrate they can act like grown-ups and get along. This was a golden opportunity to help close the divide between Left and Right.

Instead, every single commentator (I heard) took the low road. They dialed up the hate speech. They ridiculed politicians from the Left for offering assistance to, and solidarity with, their colleagues on the Right. Some even cast outright BLAME at the Left for the actions of one disturbed individual. They, all around, did their damndest to make matters worse.

Why would anyone with the power of a public pulpit seek to worsen a problem? GREED, of course! Pandering to, and enflaming hatred in, their audience is good for ratings – pure and simple. Why HELP when HATE makes you RICH?

When Senator John McCain traveled to Washington D.C. while under treatment for brain cancer, I intentionally watched FNC. The senator felt that casting his vote to open debate on a healthcare bill was important enough to make the trip. He also gave a fifteen minute address to the Senate.

In his address, McCain called on his colleagues to remember the importance of debate and working together and to return to that. Cooperation, he said, is what makes government work. He also advised ignoring the radio, TV and internet demagogues. The senator observed that their interest is not the public interest and their living comes from government's failures.

Senator McCain spoke wise words, and offered good advice. But, other than the mere mention of his showing up at the Senate, Sean Hannity, et al., did not say one word about, or air any part of, McCain's address.

Ted Koppel interviewed Sean Hannity for the program *CBS Sunday Morning*. At one point, Hannity asked if Koppel thought he was bad for the country. Koppel explained that he did, because Hannity (et al.) attracts an audience that thinks their "beliefs" are more important than "facts." Thank you, Mr. Koppel!

Donald Trump:

I apologize for disregarding the alphabetical order, but I had to save this guy for last. That is because he employs just about every demagogic strategy of manipulation that exists. By all accounts, he also does it instinctively, in addition to relentlessly.

Let us examine the 45th President of the United States of America; the phenomenon known as "The Donald."

First, let's see how he employs the most common types of propaganda – ALL of them!

<u>Ad hominem</u> (personally attacking one's opponents, rather than their arguments): "Lyin' Ted (Cruz)," "Little Marco (Rubio)," "Crazy Bernie (Sanders)," "Low Energy Jeb (Bush)," Reporters (the ones who hold him accountable – not the ones who put him on a pedestal) are all "SCUM."

<u>Ad nauseam</u> (The relentless repetition of an idea or slogan): "Make America Great Again!," "Build The Wall," "Drain The Swamp," the news media (the ones who hold him accountable – not the ones who put him on a pedestal) are all "FAKE NEWS"!

<u>Appeal to fear and Appeal to prejudice</u> (manipulate the audience by addressing their base instincts): Mexicans [in general] are "criminals," "drug dealers" and "rapists" (to justify building the wall – to "protect" *you*); Muslims [in general] are potential terrorists (to justify a "Muslim Ban" – to "protect" *you).*

<u>Disinformation</u> (falsification of public records with the intention of creating support for a cause): Claiming (ad nauseam) that "Mexico will pay for the wall" while knowing full well (as it's obvious) Mexico will NOT pay for the wall. (This was finally proven, in his eighth month in office, by phone transcripts of him *begging* Mexico's President to stop saying "Mexico will NOT pay for the wall" because it made him look bad.)

<u>Labeling and/or Name-calling</u>: See <u>ad hominem</u> (above).

<u>Flag Waving</u> (To appeal to an audience by making them believe that supporting the propagandist will make them more patriotic): The slogan "Make America Great Again!" – wall-to-wall, giant American flags across the Republican National Convention stage – accusing athletes, who protest

injustice during the (pre-game) National Anthem, of protesting *the flag*.

Lying and Deception: "Mexico will pay for the wall;" I will let you know "soon" (or) "in two weeks" (or) "any day now;" President Obama had his "wires tapped" in Trump Tower. Donald Trump (also) began his presidential run by basing it on a lie, long before officially declaring his candidacy, by his smear campaign claiming that President Obama was not born in the United States, AFTER this falsehood had long been proven untrue. (News agencies, the ones that hold him accountable – not the ones that put him on a pedestal, have calculated that Trump told at least one lie on every one of his first forty days in office. Trump has less time to lie when vacationing, golfing or posing for pictures, but lying and deception remain [probably] his favorite propaganda techniques.)

Next: How many of the "Characteristics of Demagoguery" does Trump display? (I'll bet it's oodles!)

(1) Promising security (by punishing "outgroups"): Mexicans are criminals; Muslims are terrorists; refugees are dangerous. (It's always someone else's fault.)

(2) Creating divisiveness (made to appear reasonable by the use of statistics, figures, allegations, and analytics, i.e., "The Expert Fallacy"): "I   AM YOUR VOICE!" – "I'm the only one who can fix it'!" – "YOU'RE FIRED!" (Generally, Trump has created the perception of being an "expert," over many years, by simply being a celebrity that many people [used to] "like.")

(3) Naive realism (uncomplicated descriptions) and Confirmation bias (descriptions confirm beliefs): See number (1) (above).

(4) Authoritarianism: See number (2) (above).

(5) Identity as logic (certain persons are "better" – no matter how they behave): Trump's telling his supporters to punch them [dissenters] in the face – and – telling police (who denounced him for it); don't be so nice to [alleged] law violators.

(6) Cunning projection (creates distraction in bystanders): Leakers (whistleblowers) are criminals; "LOCK HER (Hillary Clinton) UP!" – etc. (meant to distract from the demagogue's [Trump's] own bad behavior).

(7) Victimization: Trump claimed that no President was ever treated so badly. (Lincoln and Kennedy would disagree – if they could.)

(8) Metaphors: The Republican National Convention was a heart-pounding, sensory overload of "metaphors," with words like patriotic, strong, strength, law-abiding, moral and military – and phrases like "Make America Great Again!," "I AM YOUR VOICE!" and They won't take your guns away! And imagery like wall-to-wall, giant American flags.

Finally, this brings us back to the one characteristic of demagoguery that Donald Trump used in which he was able to employ all the others, in order to get elected President of the United States; number (4) Authoritarianism.

Trump knows, by both instinct and from (real) experts that he hires, the Republican "base" is more vulnerable to the arts of persuasion: Demagoguery, Prejudice, and Propaganda. This is because they are mostly-conservative and respond emotionally (remember, all propaganda appeals to the emotions rather than the intellect.)

Donald Trump's political affiliations have fluctuated over the years from Democrat to Republican and even the Reform Party. But, being a plutocrat and psychopath (oh yes, he displays ALL the traits), his only interest is *the self*.

Therefore, once he got serious, he knew he had to go "Republican," for the reasons stated in the previous paragraph.

By capitalizing on celebrity and "The Expert Fallacy" (because he "fired" people on [history's greatest propaganda tool] television for 14 years), Trump created the perception (illusion) of authority. Since Republicans (conservatives) respond emotionally and are authoritarian submissive they flocked to Trump, because he made ALL the right promises. (As proof, I can state that I have [personally] heard Trump's supporters exclaim: "He says everything we want to hear!" and [literally] refer to him as a "father figure.")

Before leaving the topic of "Demagogues," I want to mention one more example of how Donald Trump employs the device of "projection." Both before and after his election, Trump has claimed "the system is rigged!" and has boasted about how hard it was for him to win. By accusing Democrats of unfairly gerrymandering electoral districts, Trump *projected* dishonesty upon *them.* (If you care to look it up, the fact is Republicans are guilty of the unfair gerrymandering, creating an uphill battle for anyone else.) Thus, if he'd lost, Trump would have had the "rigged system" to blame. But *the mirror of truth* would have proven him wrong.

During the 2016 campaign, "Lyin' Ted (Cruz)," who is highly intelligent despite being a subversive, actually accused Donald Trump of employing "projection." But, of course, as we learned from "pornographer" Ann Coulter, most people were ...too busy and/or stupid... to understand what the hell Cruz was talking about.

All we can hope for is that the science behind the success of demagogues gets much more widespread dissemination. And that enough of the sincere, partly-progressive conservatives we love will remember that in order to change – a mind must be open. Because the science behind demagoguery demonstrates that demagogues, with their appeals to our prejudices, are the ones to be distrusted. When demagogues call their targets "un-American" they are employing the propaganda technique of "cunning projection." THEY are truly UN-AMERICAN! Their intent is to create a Conservunist utopia for their plutocrat providers, and to dismantle the America that you and I love!

Grover Norquist

The Ugly Bad:

"… government is not the solution to our problems; government is the problem." Ronald Reagan

Subversive: (1) tending to subvert or advocating subversion, especially in an attempt to overthrow or cause the destruction of an established or legally constituted government. (2) a person who adopts subversive principles or policies. Synonyms: traitorous, treacherous, seditious, destructive. *(Dictionary.com)*

According to their website, Americans for Tax Reform (ATR) was founded in 1985 by Grover Norquist "at the request of President Reagan." According to the ATR's mission statement, it opposes any tax increase as an issue of principle. Their "Taxpayer Protection Pledge" is a signed vow by lawmakers [the Congress] and office candidates by which they commit opposition to all efforts for increasing any tax on citizens or business.

This is the oath taken by those elected to both the House of Representatives and the Senate of the United States of America: "I, ___ ___, do solemnly swear (or affirm) that I will support and defend the Constitution of the United States against all enemies, foreign and domestic; that I will bear true faith and allegiance to the same; that I take this obligation freely, without any mental reservation or purpose of evasion; and that I will well and faithfully discharge the duties of the office on which I am about to enter. So help me God."

This is the ATR "Taxpayer Protection Pledge" for the Senate: "I, _____, pledge to the taxpayers of the state of, _____ and to the American people that I will: ONE, oppose any and all efforts to increase the marginal income tax rates for individuals and/or businesses; and TWO, oppose any net reduction or elimination of deductions and credits, unless matched dollar for dollar by further reducing tax rates."

This is the ATR "Pledge" for the House: "I, _____, pledge to the taxpayers of the _____ district of the state of_____, and to the American people that I will: ONE, oppose any and all efforts to increase the marginal income tax rates for individuals and/or businesses; and TWO, oppose any net reduction or elimination of deductions and credits, unless matched dollar for dollar by further reducing tax rates."

As defined by the U.S. Constitution: Only Congress shall approve the acquiring and/or disbursement of funds. Congress shall be responsible for supporting, regulating and governing the Military, and for declarations of war. Congress members shall be accountable (only) to the Congress itself for their personal, official behavior.

Therefore – since the Constitution charges that: Only Congress shall approve the acquiring and/or disbursement of funds, those funds being necessary ...for supporting, regulating and governing... AND all members of Congress "solemnly swear" to "... support and defend the Constitution of the United States against all enemies, foreign and domestic" – is signing a "pledge" that contradicts their "solemn oath" not traitorous, treacherous, seditious and destructive?

Furthermore, by not holding members of Congress "accountable" for signing a subversive pledge, aren't their fellow members also failing to uphold their sworn oath to "... defend the Constitution of the United States against all enemies, foreign and domestic"? (AM I MISSING SOMETHING HERE?)

Grover Norquist and the ATR were Ronald Reagan's gifts that keep on giving to his plutocrat patrons and their quest to solve the problem of government by causing it to go broke!

Let's look at Norquist's background and see what stellar qualities he exhibited that resulted in his being anointed by his Dear Leader.

During the struggle to end the South African apartheid policies: In an effort to gain public support in America and end sanctions, the government and companies in South Africa hired a cadre of conservative political insiders. Norquist: ...traveled to South Africa in 1985 for the "Youth for Freedom Conference" funded by South African companies. Norquist's university friend, Jack Abramoff: ...the ex-lobbyist who was found guilty of "fraud, conspiracy and tax evasion," helped launch his career by his work in South Africa. Abramoff went there in 1983 after serving as National Chair of the College Republicans. Abramoff worked with pro-apartheid groups, affiliated with the South African Bureau of Security Services. In 1986, Abramoff started the International Freedom Foundation, a supposed "think tank" later identified as a front organization for South Africa's Army, created to sabotage the global admiration of Nelson Mandela. The International Freedom Foundation had at least thirty operatives "in Washington, Johannesburg, London and Brussels" spreading propaganda for South Africa's government. As activists encouraged America to cut off South Africa's administration, Reagan's regime was working toward additional trade and collaboration. (*The Nation*, July 9, 2013)

And from The *New Yorker*, August 1, 2005: Norquist has suffered from his association with Jack Abramoff, the dubious Republican powerbroker who paid for [Congressman] Tom DeLay to fly, in 2000, to golf in Scotland. Abramoff is also known for getting millions of dollars for consulting American Indians, then writing e-mails in which he made demeaning statements about them. When the e-mails were made public by the Senate, Abramoff became noxious, and his associates' reputations became questionable. As it happens, Norquist and Abramoff have not just been associates, but good friends since university. When Abramoff ran for National Chair of the College Republicans, Norquist managed his campaign – and they have collaborated on Abramoff's American Indian political drives. Norquist strongly refutes any wrongdoing, and no evidence has shown that he's violated any laws. But his close relationship with Abramoff has damaged his stature as a rebellious dissident. Norquist has even been denounced by certain conservatives as a sell-out to big money. (I'm reminded of something my grandfather advised: "You show me who your friends are – and I'll show you who *you* are!")

The "Ronald Reagan Legacy Project" was started in 1997 by Grover Norquist. According to their website, they assure that every February 6th will be called "Ronald Reagan Day." And they advocate "landmarks, buildings, roads, etc." be named after Ronald Reagan. (Payback? No doubt. But consider this as well: What better way to keep conning the American people than to keep the name and image of their [carefully crafted by plutocrats] "patron saint" in front of their noses?)

Michael Moore (and a predecessor)

The Good:

Michael Moore is a living example of the phenomenon of backfire. In his documentary films, such as *Roger and Me, Bowling for Columbine, Fahrenheit 9/11* and *Capitalism: A Love Story,* among others, Moore carefully presents facts, logic and reason to expose the hypocrisy of plutocracy for all of us to easily see. What has it gotten him? Death threats!

Michael Moore's grandfather and both of his parents worked for General Motors. His uncle, also a GM worker, was a co-founder of the United Automobile Workers. In 1936-1937, the uncle risked his life in the "Flint Sit-Down Strike." That strike effectively put the UAW on the map.

It is worth noting here that the great Walter P. Reuther also participated in the Flint/GM Strike. In addition to that, and the beating he endured in the Ford Strike of 1937, Reuther was the target of two assassination attempts.

While a member of the Automobile Manufacturers' Association, and prior to becoming Governor of Michigan (and Mitt's daddy), George Romney called Reuther "the most dangerous man in Detroit" for the labor leader's skill in "bringing about...revolution without seeming to disturb the existing...society."

Walter Reuther was Dr. Martin Luther King, Jr.'s friend. The Detroit and Washington, DC. freedom marches of 1963 were financed by the UAW. At the D.C. march, Ruther was one of only a handful of non-African Americans to speak. Reuther and the UAW also helped Cesar Chavez and the United Farm Workers with vital funding and support in their fight for humane job conditions for agricultural workers in the southwestern United States. (Wayne State University, Walter P. Reuther Library)

Prior to World War II, Walter Reuther was a Socialist and was fired, by Ford, for campaigning on behalf of the Socialist Party candidate for President. He and his brother then traveled the world. Eventually, they found work in a Soviet automobile factory. All of the factory's equipment had been provided by Ford. (Yes, you read that right!) While in the Soviet Union, Reuther observed how Stalin's dictatorship gave Communism, and even Socialism, a bad name (much like Hitler gave all propagandists and all plutocrats a bad name). (Wayne State University, Walter P. Reuther Library)

After the second World War, Reuther left the Socialist Party. However, he retained a socialist philosophy and he rid the UAW of all communist influences. (Remember, from the definitions in Chapter I, socialism and communism are not the same. Socialism involves the people, much like democracy. Communism exploits the people, much like unregulated capitalism.)

The ethic that Walter Reuther preached and lived by was: "There is no greater calling than to serve your fellow men. There is no greater contribution than to help the weak. There is no greater satisfaction than to do it well." (Wayne State University, Walter P. Reuther Library)

In 1958, ultra-Conservative Barry Goldwater declared Reuther a "more dangerous menace than the Sputnik or anything Soviet Russia might do to America." (Krugman, Paul/2007/*The Conscience of a Liberal*/W W Norton & Company)

In 1970, at age 62, Walter Reuther, his wife and everyone else on board, was killed in a plane crash. To this day, there is suspicion that the crash was no accident and the FBI still refuses to release documents regarding it, or communications (about it) involving J. Edgar Hoover. (Parenti, Michael /1996/

Dirty Truths/City Lights Books). About two years prior to the fatal crash, Walter and his brother survived a remarkably similar plane crash.

Why would Walter Reuther, a great and exemplary American who fought tirelessly for equality, liberty and justice for all, be the target of two (if you count both plane crashes, four) assassination attempts? Could it have been because the plutocrats he fought against wanted equality, liberty and justice only for them selves?

Why would (so-called) conservatives, like George Romney and Barry Goldwater, who (ostensibly) despised Communism, refer to Walter Reuther, a man who did more to eradicate Communism than both of them put together, as "dangerous" and a "menace"? Could it have been because Reuther was successful in exposing their true intentions were to exploit the American people? Furthermore, could it have been because Walter Reuther was also successful in organizing the American people to do something about it?

Finally: Why was Walter Reuther so successful? Could it have been because he knew what his adversaries knew – but – knew how to do it better than they? That being: To appeal to people's emotions as opposed to their intellect?

With the legacy of the great Walter Reuther in his blood, Michael Moore, another great and brave American, carries the torch.

Moore is characterized as a "political activist," but he rejects the term and calls it "redundant" by saying: we all must be politically active, otherwise there is no democracy. (In other words: *YOU* ARE THE UNION!)

I'm glad we have Michael Moore, and he's had some success but not enough. Why not? Backfire. Those, like me, who already agree with his views, are encouraged by his facts, logic and reason. But those who disagree are not persuaded, as we have learned, by facts, logic or reason. Why? Because those are appeals to the intellect.

Furthermore, Moore almost always punctuates the information he presents with a call to action. Again, he's had some success but not enough. That's because neither those who agree or disagree act on appeals to the intellect. As we have learned, the only way to inspire (significant) action is to appeal to the emotions. That's how people are convinced to spend money for cigarettes that give them lung cancer and chewing tobacco that rots their teeth out.

In America today, we could use another Walter Reuther or a Dr. Martin Luther King, Jr. But we still need Michael Moore and others like him to stir the pot. What I would like to see the pot stirrers do is learn to be more emotional and less factual, logical and reasonable in their appeals. Otherwise, I'd like to see our "Michael Moores" find another Walter Reuther or Dr. Martin Luther King, Jr.

Occupy

The Good (start):

As Bill O'Reilly predicted: Americans will eventually correct our political turmoil, for one reason; the patriots outnumber the pinheads. The Occupy movement is a good beginning. It was successful in bringing attention to and causing public debate about our political turmoil. But it is yet to achieve success in correcting it. However, its early protests were only the opening salvos in the current class war. And wars, or struggles, are almost never won in the first battle. The Occupy movement will only fail if it fails to regroup and carry on the fight.

Initiatives like Occupy can trace their roots back a long way. The Occupy movement, which is widely considered to have started with "Occupy Wall Street" (OWS) in September 2011, was inspired by the "Spanish Indignados" movement of May 2011 as well as the "Arab Spring" of the previous year. Occupy was also motivated by the success of the Tea Party movement. Some Occupy protesters credit the "original" Tea Party movement (before the plutocrats who started it pulled out the stops, after it got rolling) for having values in common with Occupy (The Guardian, October 8, 2011).

Past Occupy-like struggles that were successful have been the protests against the Vietnam War, the fights for civil rights and the union battles to end worker exploitation. In addition to being examples of success, those agendas also demonstrate why the public can never rest and must always be ready to regroup and carry on the fight. Since the Vietnam War, America has entered other needless conflicts for profit. Civil rights abuses might not be as frequent but they still occur, all too often. And thanks to the rise of the plutocrats and some unions being asleep at the wheel, of course that means *us*, the exploitation of the middle (or more accurately, working) class has gotten almost as bad as it was before unions.

Going back even further, there was a struggle that many have never even heard of because it was such an embarrassment to the Government of the United States of America. Long ago, the sacrifices of those who served in our armed forces were shamefully unappreciated and the men and women who served were routinely exploited. That all changed thanks to a protest, which occurred during the Great Depression. But that successful depression-era protest serves, too, as another reminder that things will regress as soon as we let our guard down. The evidence of that is the current, abhorrent disgrace at the Veteran's Administration hospitals, and the marginalization of gender-related and women's issues in the military, by the federal government.

When I was doing media work for the TWU, I wrote an article about that mostly-forgotten armed forces protest, known as "The March of The Bonus Army." I have included it for the lessons it teaches us, and because those who were there deserve to be remembered for what they achieved and what they endured. As you read it, please pay attention to several things. First, if you leave out the dates, take notice of how I might have been writing about America today. Second, in note number one at the end, I cited my sources and I highly recommend them for further education. Third, in note number two, you will learn why this particular protest, which was probably America's first "Occupy," is so near and dear to my heart. And why, like Michael Moore, I also have a legacy in my blood that compels me to carry the torch. (See Appendix D for the full article.)

The Bonus Army had two things in its favor that the Occupy movement has been criticized for not having – leadership and a defined goal. Both groups also share a common mistake – violence.

Being comprised of (mainly) military veterans, The Bonus Army knew that any "army" requires leadership in order to have, well, order. They had elected leaders. But a visible leader (or leaders) is not a necessity – leadership is. In fact, it is often better to not have an out front leader. If the leadership does its job from behind the scenes the adversary has no one person (or persons) to focus on and attempt to neutralize in order to derail the movement. A leader who is in the spotlight is open to any number of methods of marginalization. These can include false accusations meant to discredit the leader(ship), incarceration for countless, obscure charges, and assassination.

The Bonus Army also had a defined goal – Adjusted Compensation – and they focused only on that. Many were unemployed, but they didn't (additionally) demand jobs or even Unemployment benefits (although, their actions probably helped bring about those benefits).

When "The Occupy Army" finally succumbed to the pressure to announce their demands, the list was vague and too numerous. Professor of political science Gene Sharp said: Occupy doesn't have a clear goal to achieve. The belief that economic change can be brought about by just sitting-put someplace isn't very likely. Demonstration, by itself, does not accomplish much. (Al Jazeera interview, 12/6/ 2011)

Dr. Sharp literally "wrote the book" on protest. His pamphlet, *From Dictatorship to Democracy*, is a guide on how to overthrow totalitarian regimes by non-violent means. He is a three time nominee for the Nobel Peace Prize and has written extensively about non-violent struggle. His teachings have helped resistance movements around the world. *From Dictatorship to Democracy* was distributed as a "manual" during the "Arab Spring."

On November 5, 2011, Occupy held "Bank Transfer Day." They marched on banks and other financial institutions to encourage Americans to take their money out of corporate banks and move it to credit unions or (smaller) community banks. An estimated 600,000 people, reportedly, did so. (*The Week*/November 21, 2011) The limited success of "Bank Transfer Day" was certainly due to the fact that it was a specific goal and gave people a definite strategy to employ. If Occupy had latched onto that, and ran with that singular goal, it could have been a *major* success. Then, they could have set a second singular goal, then a third. If they had, we might have been living in a much more equitable America today. The most likely reason the movement lost its direction was their (stated) aversion to defined leadership.

Violence, the mistake The Bonus and Occupy Armies had in common did not originate from them. However, it was an inevitable result of their tactics. Demonstration by legal permit is one thing, in such cases the police have even been known to protect the demonstrators. But camping out for long periods eventually becomes frustrating to both sides. And sooner or later, something gives. For a "citizen's army," the only sensible retaliation against violence from a real Army is non-violence. Back off, don't fight back, move along peaceably and live to fight another day – in a better way! Problems arise because indignation can make the urge to fight back insurmountable.

In his January 26, 1930 Declaration of Independence, Gandhi "implied" that if he had guns he would have used them. Although Gandhi might have been angry enough to have wanted to use guns, he was also smart enough to know it had to be enough guns.

More from Dr. Gene Sharp's December 2011 Al Jazeera interview: (AJ) *Sharp expresses a principal point; power is derived from the citizens' obedience. If the origins of the obedience are foiled, tyrannies can be overthrown.* (In other words, if the 99% disobey the 1%'s rules – the 1% will have no power.) (AJ) *How would you advise the Occupy movement?* (Sharp) They should study how to meaningfully change what they oppose. Economics or politics can not be changed by just sitting-put someplace.

In the interview, Dr. Sharp also spoke about the fact that he is better received when he lectures a military audience. The military take him more seriously because they understand strategy and tactics. Gene Sharp's method for struggle is not passive (as in "passive resistance") it is active, as described in his 1973 book *The Politics of Nonviolent Action*.

So, to recap the changes The Occupy Army needs to make before they regroup for the next battles: (1) They need defined leadership that understands strategy and tactics in order to frame battle plans. (2) They need to focus on one specific goal at a time and not become sidetracked. (3) They need to eliminate violence from the equation. If they are successful in attaining #1, it will take care of #'s 2 and 3.

Why couldn't they figure this out themselves? Well, the easy answer is: "Those who cannot remember the past are condemned to repeat it." The examples of Gandhi, Walter Reuther and Dr. Martin Luther King, Jr. seem to have become forgotten. And the teachings of Dr. Gene Sharp and one other man have not been sufficiently studied. That other man was a great American (and my personal) hero – Saul D. Alinsky.

Since there's good and bad in everything, I must give credit for my introduction to Saul Alinsky to, none other than, Glenn Beck. After hearing Beck "warn" his audience about the evil of Alinsky's teachings, I vetted his "facts." As I expected, I found virtually everything Beck said to be either totally untrue or twisted to make Alinsky look bad. Plutocrat puppets, like Glenn Beck, fear Saul Alinsky, to this day – 40-plus years after his death, because his teachings hold them up to *the mirror of truth!*

Then one day, I saw Mr. Alinsky's book on a shelf in a bookstore. As I'm sure it was intended to, the book's title glared at me and compelled me to pick it up. I did pick it up, thumbed through it and immediately bought it. The title is *Rules for Radicals.*

Today's radicals ought to study *Rules for Radicals* because, like the works of Dr. Gene Sharp, it is a manual on how to fight smart in order to live to fight another day.

In fact, radicals on both the Right and Left credit Alinsky's tactics as masterful. Whilst encouraging their puppets to denounce *Rules for Radicals,* Tea Party organizers and supporters provide it [as they do with *Atlas Shrugged]* to the movement's leadership. (The *Wall Street Journal*/January 23, 2012)

Saul Alinsky was in the thick of almost every struggle of the last century. He grew up during the Great Depression. He fought for the Labor movement, the Civil Rights movement and the Anti-War movement. He fought against the national disgrace of "McCarthyism." He fought against exploitative corporations and corrupt politicians. And he *always* won!

Alinsky said one of his very few regrets was not being allowed to fight the Nazis as a member of the Office of Strategic Services (OSS) during World War II. Although the organization's leader, General "Wild Bill" Donovan, thought his experience in fighting "domestic fascism" would be helpful, the Assistant Secretary of State decided he would be more valuable at home, settling labor/management disputes. (Actually, WWII was probably the only time in America's history when labor and management worked in virtual harmony. Undoubtedly, due to the existence of a common, and real, enemy.)

Radical: A person who advocates thorough or complete political or social reform (*Oxford dictionary*)

Rules for Radicals, which came out in 1971, one year before Alinsky's death, was his tactical handbook for all those who would carry on his work.

In March of 1972, Saul Alinsky spoke extensively about his life, what he'd seen, done, experienced, learned and had to teach us, in an interview with writer Eric Norden for *Playboy* magazine:

Alinsky on why we have lost the will to fight:

When injustice is overwhelming, people rarely rebel, they usually give up.

The solution is in building strong local movements that can become national, to eventually achieve your goals. This takes time and effort, which discourages many big-talking radicals.

Life, itself, is war. It is the ongoing struggle to change the status quo that rejuvenates society and energizes hope for progress toward new ideals in us. "The struggle itself is the victory."

"Prosperity makes cowards of us all." Once you get on top, your desire is to remain there. Your perceived freedom becomes your prison. (To many [maybe most] of us, reaching "the top" means a TV on which to watch football on Sunday, beer in the fridge and a cell-phone on which to order in pizza. Once that "prosperity" is achieved it is forgotten that "the struggle itself is the victory," then the will to fight is lost. And: It is no accident!)

Alinsky on tactics (that work):

People don't get ahead from charity. They must fight the establishment for it. The liberal notion of "reconciliation" is baloney. "Reconciliation" only means this: If you get enough power, your opponent must reconcile with you. You must have organization to force your opponent to meet your demands and make good on them. If you're too soft, you might as well quit. This was the white liberals' fatal error, thinking altruism could change society. That's delusional. Nothing can be compromised until you have the power to force it.

If you successfully get your opponent to negotiate, then you must bring a solution* to the table. (*A defined goal)

Originality is the secret to tactics that work. First, it keeps your activists from losing interest. Tactics can become stale from overuse. Repetitive and unimaginative tactics eventually turn people off, no matter how egregious their maltreatment is, or how combative they are. Also, your opponent can anticipate your moves and make counter-plans, unless you continually change yours.

One day, an executive at a large company showed me the plans for their fancy new headquarters. He pointed out the spot that would be a "sit-in hall," which would have seats, beverages and reading materials. He said protesters would just be escorted there and could stay as long as they liked. That was when I knew the era of sit-ins was over. (If Occupy had read the *Playboy* interview, or studied *Rules for Radicals*, they might have reconsidered the sit-in strategy.) If you want success, you need to keep creating innovative and superior techniques. A city once told us they lacked funds for trash pickup when we complained that it was insufficient. So we collected our own garbage and dumped it on the alderman's lawn. In 48 hours, regular trash collection began.

To screw your opponent, you must first entice your allies. (When Occupy held "Bank Transfer Day" they enticed their allies by giving them something concrete to do. And they won a victory!) For me, a primary rule is never appeal with abstractions ...appeal to "self-interest." (This, too, reinforces why "Bank Transfer Day" worked.) Alinsky went on to say this strategy also succeeds with the adversary. When it becomes apparent that concession will be more economical than continuing to oppress the radical element, the adversary will concede; it's in their self-interest.

In America, no radicals have the force to take on the police in armed conflict, let alone the military. It's lunacy to think power is in a gun barrel when your enemy has all the guns. (This is another reason why the sit-in no longer works. Once they get tired of looking at you, they will turn the guns on you. [O]r as was seen in the case of Occupy, the batons and pepper-spray.)

Power isn't in what the authorities have – it's in what you believe they have.

From *Rules for Radicals:* Tactics' cardinal rule is: Power isn't just in what your side has, but also in what the other side believes your side has. Power always comes from two leading origins, money and people. Without money, the Have-Nots must rely on their own mass to attain power. A great movement asserts itself with great tactics. To oppose the skill and polish of the establishment, the Have-Nots always had to fight their way. (Power comes in the form of either *money* or *people*. As Gandhi, Walter Reuther, Saul Alinsky and Dr. Martin Luther King, Jr. demonstrated; with a large enough force employing superior strategy and insurmountable tactics, *people* have the greater power and *always* win.)

Alinsky on how power corrupts and why "The struggle itself is the victory":

Take the American Revolutionary War; Samuel Adams was its most committed leader. But as soon as the war was won, Adams turned into a reactionary tyrant. To caution the public, he demanded the execution of all the leaders of Shays' Rebellion. Adams was entitled to revolt, but no one was entitled to do the same to Adams. Even Gandhi; not long after India became independent, he gave in to making passive resistance illegal, and he gave up his ethic of nonviolence to back a military takeover in Kashmir. Goa and Pakistan eventually met the same fate. Again and again, enthusiastically rebellious defenders of freedom become the first to crush the rights of, and even kill, the rebels who come next. ("The struggle itself is the victory" because the struggle never ends. Once we think "we've won" all is lost.)

Alinsky on an American disgrace:

McCarthyism's spread made radical actions more and more difficult. Back then, anyone that challenged the system got labeled a Communist. The pressure made the radical movement come apart.

(Eric Norden for *Playboy*) *Were you affected, personally, in the McCarthy era?* (Alinsky) Not personally, but the overall uneasiness made it hard to organize. All in all, McCarthy hurt the nation terribly. Prior to McCarthy, each generation saw radicals; ready to fight the establishment. McCarthy turned America into a wasteland of fear. Liberals who weren't totally committed to the cause ran and hid. A lot betrayed their friends to save their own hides. (Democrat, at the time, and "president of a union," Ronald Reagan, not only saved his hide but prospered by joining the followers of McCarthy and their progeny.) The most ferocious radicals from the 1930's ran scared and snuck away; leaving a cowardly heritage for themselves. Only a handful of worn-down dissidents were left to pass the torch to the next revolutionaries. Kids today are right when they mock their parents for copping-out.

Alinsky on why we the people need to stick together and why it pays to do your homework:

The most sorrowful part is if dissidents and progressives had only stuck together we would have stopped McCarthy cold. One time, in the 1950's, he sent some of his people to see me. They wanted me to provide them with a list of my associates, otherwise they would have me subpoenaed and McCarthy would ruin my reputation. I laughed right at them and then I threw them out. But first I said, "You think I give a damn about my reputation?" I told them to go ahead, subpoena me; I won't take the Fifth either. He can make me give yes and no answers, but when the reporters get hold of me, he can't prevent me from telling them how he sought out support from the Communists when he ran for the Senate in 1946. You can tell McCarthy I said "go to hell." They were high and mighty when they walked in, they thought I would grovel, but they walked out pale and shaken. I kept organizing through the entire 1950's with no trouble from D.C., but I did catch quite a bit of static from local police.

Alinsky on the mentality of plutocrats:

I once was at a luncheon with several corporate presidents who wanted to "know their enemy." One guy told me that I seemed OK, and asked; but why do you view everything as a power struggle instead of with kindliness, consideration and harmony? I answered; I'll follow your example when you and your company approach your competitors with kindliness, consideration and harmony rather than being out to cut their throats. The table went silent, and the topic changed.

Alinsky on propaganda, the other, and thinking about what you're thinking:

The right wing gives the people scapegoats for their troubles; African Americans, gays, the commies – and should they win, America will be the first totalitarian nation with an anthem commemorating "the land of the free and the home of the brave." But we won't give up without a fight that I believe we'll win. We'll make the middle class aware of their true enemies: the plutocrats who pull the strings and destroy the nation, those who really benefit from, so-called, economic reform. And when they focus on that bull's-eye, it's really gonna hit the fan.

Alinsky's premonitions on the America we live in today, because we've let our guard down:

(Eric Norden for *Playboy*) *You appear optimistic. But many radicals and liberals appear fearful that we're entering a time of new repression and invasion of privacy.* (Repression: The Department of Homeland Security? Invasion of privacy: The National Security Agency?) (Eric Norden for *Playboy*) *Are these exaggerated fears, or is the nation truly in danger of turning into a police state?* (Alinsky) That danger certainly exists, the nationwide infatuation with law and order shows that. But you can't just give in to despair; what to do is go out and rebel against this fascism; build a mass movement to promote progressiveness. Otherwise, your whining about a police state will become self-fulfilling. That is one reason why all my efforts are now being directed toward the organizing of the middle class. That is where the nation's future will be decided. I'm certain that as soon as the middle class understands their true enemies, the plutocrats that pull their political-puppets' strings, they will become one of the greatest forces for social change America has ever seen. There is a second rebellion bubbling in the middle class. They are confused, scared and voiceless. They are desperately seeking options and hope. They feel powerless due to fear and frustration – that can send them into a political frenzy and make them demonic, pushing them over to the right, and that can make them vulnerable to a phony, knight-in-shining-armor who promises the return of yesterday's bygone beliefs. (These premonitions should give you the chills! We *are* confused, scared and voiceless. We do seek options and hope, and we feel powerless because of fear and frustration. That fear and frustration *has* pushed us over to the right, and made us vulnerable to a phony, knight-in-shining-armor who promises the return of yesterday's bygone beliefs – TWICE! Both Ronald Reagan and Donald Trump exploited our fear and frustration; promising the return of yesterday's bygone beliefs by vowing to "Make America Great Again!" and to be "…YOUR VOICE!" They both also gave us scapegoats for our troubles; to divert focus from our true enemies. I told you radicals on both the Right and Left credit Alinsky's tactics as masterful. Didn't I?)

Alinsky on why *we the people* are a sleeping giant:

The middle class is confused between its brainwashing and its circumstances. Instinctively, the middle class wants to maintain and glorify the status quo, at the same time they see proof all around that the status quo has lied and used them.

The middle class live in a world that is totally oriented toward mass-media; they watch the TV news and see astonishing hypocrisy, deception and plain stupidity in the country's leadership as well as the corruptness and collapse of all the nation's foundations, from law-enforcement to the judicial system to even the White House.

Alinsky's strategy to wake up the giant:

(In *Rules for Radicals*, Saul Alinsky noted that the best tactics sometimes come about by "accident." He quoted Abraham Lincoln as having said "My policy is to have no policy." Three years later Lincoln followed this up in a letter to a friend, saying, "I have been controlled by events."

Alinsky explained that what Lincoln meant was one must be *open-minded*. When certain strategies or tactics become ineffective, one must be fluid and search for the next chink in the enemy's armor.

In the 1960's, Rochester, New York was a company town controlled by the Eastman Kodak Corporation. After a series of bloody race riots, Alinsky was invited to Rochester to negotiate with Kodak on behalf of Rochester's black community. The goal was to get Kodak, which had routinely exploited the town's blacks, to recognize their community organization as a legitimate bargaining agent. Things went nowhere for months upon months. Then one day, Alinsky stumbled upon his greatest strategy: "Tactic Proxy."

His idea was to gain entry into an upcoming Kodak shareholders meeting, only for the opportunity to ridicule the company in public. In order to do that, his people needed to either hold Kodak stock or voting proxies, so he began a campaign to ask for Kodak proxies to be assigned to his organization. As the proxies rolled in, what he had stumbled upon became apparent to Alinsky.

Today, the lessons learned in Rochester, fifty years ago, are more glaring than ever. And "Tactic Proxy" is more necessary than ever. The plutocrats of today are no longer motivated from demonstrations by legal permit. They just watch them as entertainment. They are no longer concerned with sit-ins. They just send in the troops. And they have even become so callous and dissolute, they no longer respond to ridicule. However, in his battle with Kodak, Saul Alinsky revealed the obvious. The most effective way, besides refusing to vote for their puppet-politicians, to gain back what has been stolen from *us* by kleptocrats is to hit them in the only place they feel pain, then, now and always – THE WALLET!)

I spoke to the Unitarian-Universalist Association to request the proxies on their Kodak stock, to get access to the shareholders' meeting. The Unitarians gave the proxies for all 5,620 shares, worth more than $700,000. The news quickly traveled across the country. Private shareholders started to send us their proxies. Other churches said they were ready to follow the example of the Unitarians. By shear accident, we hit a tactical jackpot. As politicians watched major churches give us their proxies, they feared we might get their votes, too. A large church represents a large voter block. Congressmen and senators, who previously wouldn't answer the phone when we called, began showing interest in my appeal for investigations into Kodak's hiring procedures.

As we received more and more proxies, Kodak started to feel the heat; and other companies did, too. Top executives started approaching me, seeking to discover my plans. The establishment was more nervous than I had ever seen them, this assured me we'd found the key to the gate protecting the private sector from its public obligations. Obviously, Kodak was also assured, because they quickly capitulated. Kodak was frightened, and Wall Street was frightened.

(Eric Norden for *Playboy*) *Are you saying you think you can get so many proxies that you can use them to control a big company?* (Alinsky) Of course not, forget that "people's capitalism" baloney, controlling-shares in any big company are held by a select few who would never cooperate. It's even possible to get a few people elected to a corporate board, but we aren't even concerned with that.

Four or five people on a twenty-five-member board would be voted down by management, over and over. We want proxies to serve in pressuring big business, politically and socially, to expose their fraud and deception.

Tactic Proxy is also a way to get the middle class participating in revolutionary causes. Rather than running corporate recruiters off their campuses, student activists could get together and demand the school assign them their corporate share proxies. Of course, they would refuse, but a couple might give in, still, it would be a good organizing matter. And lazy liberals can have clear consciences by handing over their proxies, and doing nothing else.

Proxies can open the door to other ways of organizing the middle class. Using proxies on a grand scale might democratize Wall Street, and bring about changes in corporate, overseas practices, which would then trigger substantial changes in America's foreign policies. There are no limits to the potential of Tactic Proxy. While he served as an advisor to Nixon, Pat Moynihan told me Tactic Proxy meant revolution, and they would never allow me to get away with it. Yes, it does mean revolution, a bloodless revolution, and we're going to get away with it, in the coming years. My plan is to devote the remainder of my life to this cause. This will be hard, but it can be won. You must never give up, regardless of how bleak things look at the time. "I love this goddamn country, and we're going to take it back."

Alinsky on (his) death:

Well, I tend not to worry about it. In my type of work, death frequently arrives "suddenly and unexpectedly."

(Unfortunately, Senator Moynihan was right. The Battle of Rochester was the one and only time Saul Alinsky was able to employ Tactic Proxy and get away with it. Three months after he gave this interview, Saul Alinsky died "suddenly and unexpectedly" from a massive heart attack. He was 63 years old.)

"Our crown has already been bought and paid for. All we have to do is wear it." James Baldwin.

We stand upon the shoulders of radicals. Exploited and oppressed people were liberated by radicals, like Gandhi, Lech Walesa and Nelson Mandela. America was built by radicals – such as Saul D. Alinsky, Walter P. Reuther, Dr. Martin Luther King, Jr., The Continental Army, The Bonus Army, and today, The Occupy Army – who "love[d] this goddamn country." We owe our crown to the radicals who devoted, and all too often sacrificed, their lives for us. "Our crown has already been bought and paid for" by radicals. It is being stolen, piece by piece, by subversives. Our duty as Americans is to continually fight to protect our right to "wear it."

Police

The Good:

Police: The civil force of a national or local government, responsible for the prevention and detection of crime and the maintenance of public order. (*Oxford Dictionary*)

Credited as the father of modern policing, Sir Robert (now you know why British cops are called "Bobbies") Peel authored the eponymously referred to Peelian principles, which set down basic guidelines for ethical policing: (1) All police officers should have an identifying number, to assure answerability for their actions. (2) Lack of crime, not frequency of arrests, should be the measure of police effectiveness. (3) More than anything else, a responsible figure of authority understands that trustworthiness and accountableness are essential. Thus, we get Peel's most quoted principle: "The police are the public and the public are the police." (From an *About.com* article: "The History of Modern Policing – How the Modern Police Force Evolved" by Timothy Roufa, Criminology Careers Expert at *About.com* – Captain/ Assistant Chief Training Officer at Florida Highway Patrol)

The Bad:

Well, having a force to detect and prevent crime and maintain public order serves a good purpose. And Sir Robert Peel's principles are good guidelines for such a force. Furthermore, such a force is necessary in our modern world. But since there is good and bad in everything, let us employ logic and reason to determine what the negative aspect might be.

Simply, the answer is the fact that such a force is "necessary." Therefore, it can be logically stated that a police force – or, for that matter, a military, a spy agency or any other type of security force – is a necessary evil. This is not meant to imply that police are necessarily evil. What is evil is the fact they are necessary. In other words, in a perfect world (one without evil) we would have no need for police.

The Ugly:

In order to be effective, police must, obviously, be granted certain authority or power. A side-effect of power is the abuse of power. And since we do not live in a world without evil, therein lays "the ugly."

Moreover, the ugly does not only emanate from police abusing their power in the line of duty. It also stems from the fact they are "the civil force of a national or local government." As such, the police are often misused, by government direction, to abuse their power.

There is no need, here, to cite specific instances of police, or the military, abusing their power. The list is long and well known. Protesters, demonstrating legally and peacefully, have been beaten, fire-hosed, tear gassed, pepper-sprayed, even shot and killed. The WWI veterans of The Bonus Army, Labor demonstrators, civil rights marchers, anti-war protestors and the Occupy "sitters" have all had their First Amendment guarantee of "... the right of the people peaceably to assemble, and to petition the Government for a redress of grievances" violated by the abuse of power.

Truth be told, I have nothing against police. In fact, I have several family members who are police officers. I'm even related to an FBI Agent (I think?). My only disappointment is the fact we live in a world that needs police.

I also have nothing against the military. Remember, my entire generation, all of whom are thirty years older than I, fought in WWII. My father fought in WWI and, after having been shot at by the U.S. Army (See: Appendix D), fought again in WWII. The only time I have a problem with the American military is when they shoot at Americans!

At this point, you might be thinking: "Here it comes! He has nothing against the police or the military. He's going to say his problem is with the government misusing the police and the military." Wrong. The problem is with *us*.

For two hundred and some-odd years, we have abused *ourselves* by electing plutocrat-puppet, major party politicians who exploit us by abusing their governmental authority to misuse the police and military.

The abuse will only stop when we start thinking about what we're thinking and acting in our own best interest. The plutocracy will only end, and the political reform will only begin, when we start voting for Independent representatives who are on our side and not obligated to the plutocracy. If we "love this goddamn country" and want to "take it back" we must resurrect our American legacy. We must all become radicals!

Richard Trumka

The (not quite) Good (enough):

In *Rules for Radicals*, Saul Alinsky told the story of a Catholic seminary near his Chicago home. As an annual tradition, members of the graduating class made it a point to visit him on the day before they were to be ordained as priests. Their discussion was mostly about ways to employ organizational strategy and tactics in order to better serve their calling.

One particular year, the group of soon-to-be-priests expressed concern that once assigned to parishes they would become swept up in the old ways and be coerced into maintaining the status quo. And they asked Alinsky: How do we uphold our Christian values, all the ways in which we hope to make changes to the system?

Alinsky answered: Easy, when you get out there, just decide if your desire is to be a bishop or a priest, the rest will take care of itself.

Other observations Alinsky made were: "Prosperity makes cowards of us all." Once you get on top, your desire is to remain there. Your perceived freedom becomes your prison. And: Too many eager and scrappy labor leaders …become satisfied and sluggish.

It is for those reasons I see current AFL-CIO President Richard Trumka (who I have observed but have never met), as well as many other Labor leaders (who I have personally worked with), as being good – but not quite good enough. Once they became "bishops" they forgot their calling.

Let us start with the good that Richard Trumka has done.

As President of the United Mine Workers, Trumka campaigned against racism (he still does, today) and won the Letelier-Moffitt Human Rights Award in 1990, for his efforts against apartheid in South Africa (while Ronald Reagan and his acolytes supported apartheid [racism] and still do, today).

In UMW strikes he led, Trumka encouraged civil disobedience and other non-violent tactics. When asked, by the Associated Press during one strike, in 1993, about the possibility of the eruption of violence in response to the hiring of "replacement workers" (scabs) in strikes, Trumka said: If you light a fire and stick your hand in it, you'll probably get burned. He also said, I don't mean I will burn you, I just mean logic dictates it. Logic dictates that if you bring in scabs during a strike, lots of things can happen. Confrontation is one of them. No, I don't want it, but yes, I think it can happen. The Associated Press reported that he was not threatening violence, and noted that UMW staff had spent "thousands of man-hours trying to prevent anything from happening ... to our members or by our members." (Eugene Register-Guard/September 3, 1993)

President Harry S. Truman famously said "the buck stops here." As a strike leader, any impropriety from his side will be laid at Richard Trumka's doorstep. Furthermore, the opportunity to use any impropriety to discredit Trumka (the leader) will be seized upon by the opposition. Even if the leader is on record, like Richard Trumka, denouncing the impropriety, the opposition will employ "Lying and Deception" in their attempts to neutralize the leader, as they do with Richard Trumka.

In 1993, an "impropriety" occurred that the opponents of Richard Trumka, and of the working class, seized upon. A union striker shot and killed a scab.

Plutocrats and their puppet pundits regularly and continually bring up that incident as evidence that Richard Trumka, the AFL-CIO, unions and every unionized worker are all violent gangsters. They like to use the word "thug" in referring to Trumka and "goons" in describing working people. The scab that was killed is portrayed as a "martyr" who was murdered while simply trying to provide for his family. Cleverly, the plutocracy spins the incident to infer that the scab died because he had "moral values," at the hands of "immoral" thugs and goons. By examining the facts, without bias, *the mirror of truth* shows who's values were actually moral, and who was (and is) selfish and immoral.

Before all else, the killing of the scab was, simply and undeniably, murder and is to be denounced. That being established, when thousands of one's neighbors are fighting to provide for their own families, is it not selfish and immoral to think (and act) only about you? This fact does not excuse murder. But it does exemplify Richard Trumka's warning to any would-be scabs: If you light a fire and stick your hand in it, you'll probably get burned. No matter how herculean the efforts to prevent trouble might be – trouble might happen. If one spits in the faces of one's neighbors – one of one's neighbors might spit back.

Furthermore, the selfish mindset of a scab is actually self-defeating. The 1993 strike was eventually won. And the union maintained their hard-fought rights and benefits, which the employer was attempting to illegally take away. If the short-sighted and selfish scabs had been successful in helping the employer break the strike they would have been "rewarded" with lower paying jobs with fewer benefits, no workplace rights and no job security.

Richard Trumka was elected president of the AFL-CIO after the retirement of John Sweeney in 2009. He got off to a good start and was certainly more proactive than Mr. Sweeney, who held office during my tenure in the Labor movement.

In 2010, the AFL-CIO backed demonstration marches in New York and Washington D.C. Mr. Trumka, personally, led the April 29 march down Broadway in New York's financial district to "Make Wall Street Pay" for going right back to business-as-usual after taking $700 billion in taxpayer bailouts. I traveled to New York from Texas to join the "March on Wall Street." We marched – the Wall Street plutocrats enjoyed the show – everybody went home – and nothing changed.

In his first few years as AFL-CIO President, Richard Trumka could be found on television often. He made the rounds of the Sunday morning news shows. He joined discussion panels on PBS and C-SPAN to address the exploitation of the working class and Labor's role in stopping that exploitation. And he always passed "The Judge Judy Test," he made sense. And nothing changed.

Today, I can't remember the last time I saw Richard Trumka on, history's greatest propaganda tool, television. I also cannot remember the last time the AFL-CIO sponsored a protest. They did "endorse" the Occupy movement, which was good – but not quite good enough. It is for these reasons, I tend to feel that Mr. Trumka, and the Labor movement as a whole, has forgotten "the struggle itself is the victory."

I am not, and cannot, stating as fact that Mr. Trumka, or any other Labor leader, has forgotten his calling in order to protect his position. At least, I hope that is not the case. But as Saul Alinsky warned, it is something for a person in his position to look in the mirror and ask himself.

There is another phenomenon that Alinsky warned about, which might be at play: When injustice is overwhelming, people rarely rebel, they usually give up. It might be that after endorsing, demonstrating, protesting, marching and making sense for five years and seeing nothing change, frustration has made Richard Trumka lose "the fire."

What makes good radicals, like Richard Trumka, into great radicals, like George Washington, Abraham Lincoln, Walter Reuther, Dr. Martin Luther King, Jr., Lech Walesa and Saul Alinsky, is the ability to devise new strategies when the old ones no longer work.

Since demonstrations, sit-ins, protest marches, ridicule or even making sense no longer work, the time has come to relegate those strategies to history. Today, a workforce going on strike against a corporation is practically suicide. They might as well just quit their jobs and look for new ones. Ever since Reagan created the template, by firing all the striking members of PATCO legally, the tactic has been repeated by corporations regularly – illegally. The point has been reached when Richard Trumka, or "Labor," or "the working class," or *we*, needs to fight fire with fire – MONEY!

Economic protest is the only way to get through to those who only care about economics. And the most beautiful aspect of economic protest is that it's perfectly legal. As such, just the threat of it makes plutocrats soil their pinstriped pants! Saul Alinsky brought not only Kodak Corporation but all of Wall Street to their knees by just letting them get wind of it.

What if the AFL-CIO had given the Occupy movement more substantial support? What if they had offered free transportation on "Bank Transfer Day," to anyone willing to make a withdrawal? The odds are high that "Bank Transfer Day" might not have even had to happen. Most likely, if the big, commercial banks had known in advance they were going to face a legal "run" of epic size they would have headed it off by becoming more "customer friendly."

What if "Bank Transfer Day" had been followed up with "Cut Up Your Credit Card Day," encouraging people to transfer all their credit card accounts from the big banks to credit unions? The likely outcome would have been that the interest rates would have gone down before anyone took out their scissors.

What if the leaders of my union, the Transport Workers, had taken my suggestion to use The Occupy Army to legally gum up the works at American Airlines? (See: Appendix C) If the TWU President, at the time, had decided to "… go out and 'occupy' something," instead of just say it, AA's plutocrats would have felt the pain in their wallet and been more responsive to their stated "most valuable asset," their people. And that particular TWU President as well as many of his officers, all of whom came from the Airline Division, would have been praised instead of booted out in the next election and replaced with leadership from the more progressive, and aggressive, Transit Division.

What might happen if the American Labor movement started buying commercial time on radio and, of course, television to educate the middle class as to how they are being exploited and offer concrete strategies, tactics and help for fighting back?

What might happen if *we* started employing Saul Alinsky's "Tactic Proxy," to compel the democratization of corporate America?

What would happen would be peaceful, legal and effective revolution. No more marching or camping out in the streets. No more need to endure violence. The Occupy Army's parents and grandparents could employ these strategies, which are easy, convenient and work better as well as faster.

All we need is leadership to educate, motivate, publicize, strategize, set tactics and identify specific goals. That's it! But seriously, it will be a lot of hard work. And no one, such as Richard Trumka, could do it alone, nor should he. We don't want anything "sudden or unexpected" to happen to our leader. However, someone like Richard Trumka is in a position to create a team of anonymous leaders to take up where Saul Alinsky left off, 40-plus years ago.

Technology

The (simultaneously) Good, Bad and Ugly:

Bill O'Reilly, the man who inspired me to write this book, said about technology; the increasing reliance on machines to do our thinking is dangerous. His particular concern is about the way we are becoming over-reliant on technology in the quest for quick answers, solutions and rewards. O'Reilly's concern is something we all should be worried about. Our zeal for having everything "now" makes us more vulnerable to manipulation than ever before in history, simply because we don't want to take the time to think about what we're thinking.

I am not implying, and I'm sure Mr. O'Reilly isn't either, a legion of laptop-Luddites should go around taking sledge-hammers to computers. Technology is somewhat like politics, it's a process, a tool, a means to an end. Technology in itself, like politics, is not bad. The abuse of it is bad. The misuse of it is ugly.

Webster's dictionary defines technology as: "the use of science in industry, engineering, etc., to invent useful things or to solve problems." By that definition all technology is good, and rightly so.

When early humans had only their hands to rip into a dead animal, the invention of stone tools became the height of technology. The misuse of that technology, to stab another early human, would have been bad, not the technology itself.

When cave-men discovered fire, it became the height of technology. Its use for light, warmth and cooking was all good. The misuse of fire to burn down someone else's cave (well, you know what I mean) would have been bad, not fire itself.

The invention of the gun, so we no longer had to chase dinner and bludgeon it, was the height of technology. Used properly, the technology of the gun is good. The abuse of that technology by the gun manufacturers and the NRA, who want everyone to buy a gun whether they know how to use it or not, is bad. The misuse of that technology, by maniacs who take advantage of the NRA's abuse of it, is ugly. The NRA is correct when they say "guns don't kill people – people kill people," which is further evidence of their hypocritical abuse.

Today, when we talk about technology we're almost always referring to the current height of technology, computers and other electronic devices. The good in electronic technology is limitless. If not for the computer, this book would have taken me fourteen years to write, instead of four (excluding time spent earning a living and doing the chores). Having a computer is practically like having the Library of Congress in your house!

At this point, it will be helpful for me to describe my process in writing this book. Besides gathering information and inspiration from reading other books and articles, as well as watching a copious and varied amount of television programming, and listening to my fellow Americans' concerns every day, 80% to 90% of my research was done on my computer.

Once I identified any subject I felt I needed to write about, the first place I went was *Google*. Nine times out of every ten, *Google* steered me to *Wikipedia,* so I started going directly there. *Wikipedia* gets criticized, mainly, because its content can (apparently) be altered by just about anyone. That is why I checked out every citation and reference given in every article. Then I checked out every citation and reference given in every citation and reference, through as many layers as possible. I'm not only including this as evidence that "I did my homework" to ensure the accuracy of my facts. I am also saying it to illustrate the benefit and convenience of computer technology, in addition to all the bus fare it saves! (By the way, I have become a devotee of *Wikipedia,* which is not-for-profit. And I send them a donation every Christmas, the only time they solicit.)

But there's good and bad in everything. If I had not vetted everything I learned from *Wikipedia,* by going to the actual sources and checking *their* sources, and had inadvertently included any untruths, it would have been (my) bad. (Just for the record, in all the fact-checking I did, I did not uncover any inaccuracies contained in *Wikipedia.* I'm not saying that, unequivocally, none exist, only that I did not find any – not once.) This also illuminates the bad of wanting everything "now." Remember: As opposed to accepting "facts" automatically, as offered by the first source we get them from, it is safer to be skeptical – even if (maybe especially if [?]) that source proclaims to side with our personal ideology.

Said another way, by writer Katherine Dunn in the *New Republic* in 1993, as quoted in Bernard Goldberg's 2002 book *Bias:* Keeping good folks accountable doesn't imply they're bad folks. Be skeptical of both sides, even if one of them is your mother.

Although the abuse of technology, in the desire to have everything "now" can be bad, the misuse of it, by either the good folks or the bad folks, can be ugly. An example is the apparently limitless spying on private citizens that the National Security Agency (NSA) has been exposed for doing.

The debate about this issue runs positive as well as negative. Should a government spy on everyone, with or without just cause, ostensibly to protect us? Why should anyone who feels they have nothing to hide worry about it? The Fourth Amendment to the United States Constitution might hold the answers: "The right of the people to be secure in their persons, houses, papers, and effects, against unreasonable searches and seizures, shall not be violated, and no Warrants shall issue, but upon probable cause, supported by Oath or affirmation, and particularly describing the place to be searched, and the persons or things to be seized."

Not using technology for good is almost as ugly as misusing it for bad. For instance, take voting. I own stock in several corporations. Every year, I receive mailed proxies with instructions on how I may vote my shares. Ever since computers became commonplace, voting "online" is always an option. If online voting is considered secure enough for voting corporate shares why isn't it, also, for voting in political elections? Might the answer be that certain parties (with power) want to make it as difficult as possible for certain *others* to vote? (For the record, I always vote my corporate shares against every proposal a Board of Directors recommends voting for and vice-versa, just because I can. And because Boards of Directors, like most of those with power, are only interested in their interests – not mine.)

The game-changer might be found in the technology of social media, as it was during the "Arab Spring." Thousands of ordinary citizens coordinated their efforts, without the need for a vulnerable, out-front leader, and changed (for better or worse) the structures of entire countries.

In his 2013 book *Citizenville: How to Take the Town Square Digital and Reinvent Government,* former mayor of San Francisco and California lieutenant governor, Gavin Newsom postulated: "...with the advent of social-networking technology, the leader is us."

XII

Preaching to the Choir

"I see your point – BUT!"

I realized at a pretty early age that it's impossible, not *almost* impossible but *impossible,* to change someone else's mind. To one degree or another, most of us realize this. That's why people in the "Bible Belt," where I live now, coined the phrase "preaching to the choir." And the less reverent in New York, where I grew up, say they sometimes feel like they're "talking to a wall."

A mind can only be changed by its owner and only if its owner is open-minded. That is, unfortunately, not the case most of the time. We have all experienced instances when we *knew* we were right but could not convince someone else to understand because they *believed* they were right. It is always tremendously frustrating. But the frustration can be lessened and, maybe, we can have more success in our efforts to persuade if we keep in mind the science behind it.

Motivated reasoning, backfire and appeals to the emotions are all examples of "preaching to the choir." And they work, as we have learned, because we don't actually "think" we are right – we *feel* we are right. As research professor Brendan Nyhan explained, "it's absolutely threatening to admit you're wrong."

That's why many who disagree with things I have written in this book will disagree even more fervently and maybe even hate me for writing them, regardless of my efforts to back up my arguments with facts. Remember, facts are overridden by emotions and the only way to override emotions is to have an open mind. Having learned this has relieved much of my frustration. I don't expect or even hope to persuade everyone who reads this book to agree with, or even give any serious consideration to, my views – only the open-minded – those who are prepared to think about what they're thinking.

Therefore, I will now declare who my team is. It's not the Liberals, although I usually side with them. And it's not the radicals, although (when their cause is just) I praise, and often join, them. My team is the open-minded – those who are not threatened by being wrong.

A few years ago, I wrote the following in a letter to a close relative with an authoritarian personality: "Sometimes I am right and sometimes I am wrong, but when I am wrong I admit it, for one simple reason; I do not like to be wrong."

A secondary factor that makes it threatening to be wrong is what Mark Twain said: "A man cannot be comfortable without his own approval." No one can effectively function with the knowledge they are wrong. Think of the most evil figures you can from all of history – Caligula, Hitler, Stalin, take your pick. Every single one believed himself to be a "nice guy" and "right." No one with common sense would accuse any of them of being open-minded.

The open-minded, however, are not threatened by being wrong. They have no need to justify their wrong-thinking or wrong-doing, even after being proven wrong. They can only be comfortable by admitting they are wrong and moving on. Know-it-alls become more convinced they are right when shown they are wrong. The open-minded are grateful when shown they are wrong. In both cases, the reason is the same – no one likes to be wrong. The difference is in how they approach the problem.

The third factor, we learned about, which makes it intimidating to be wrong was: The more fearful people are – the easier they are to manipulate. And that is, of course, why demagogues keep their followers fearful and "preach to the choir." That way, their followers, who are listening without thinking about what they're thinking, will be easier to manipulate. The more insecure or threatened we feel the less likely we are to listen to dissenting opinions.

In his book, *Pinheads and Patriots,* Bill O'Reilly said: Pinheads want to hurt those who disagree with them. Patriots, conversely, are courageous in stating their beliefs and engaging in debate with respect. Consider those you know – and consider yourself. "Where do you stand?"

None of us could have said it better! The know-it-all, who is threatened by disagreement, easily becomes, well, disagreeable. The open-minded, on the other hand, respect the opinions of others because they are secure in the knowledge that one can only be right if one does not always *insist* on being right. Think about what you're thinking. And indeed, think about Mr. O'Reilly's question: "Where do you stand?"

XIII

Last Rights

"Get up, stand up, Stand up for your rights. Get up, stand up, Don't give up the fight." Bob Marley

Right: (1) That which is morally correct, just, or honorable (2) A moral or legal entitlement to have or obtain something or to act in a certain way (*Oxford dictionary*)

In this penultimate chapter, I want to discuss rights. There are all kinds of rights: Constitutional rights, legal rights, moral rights, human rights, civil rights and, of course, right and wrong. Everything we have learned so far can destroy them, if we allow it, or protect them, if we are vigilant. Either way, it's our choice. But remember, the latter takes *work*. If we won't do the work, those with the power to abuse our rights will eventually give our freedom the Last Rites!

A good right to re-visit first would be the First Amendment of the U.S. Constitution, specifically, the part about freedom of speech. Remember what Noam Chomsky said: To embrace free speech you must embrace the free speech of ideas you don't agree with.

Let's begin with some good news. Since there's good and bad in everything, I would be remiss to not give credit where credit is due. Despite my earlier, scathing review of Glenn Beck, he later said something (in 2014) that, I think, deserves praise. Precisely, he spoke out against plans for U.S. re-involvement in Iraq to thwart its possible takeover by terrorists. Whether we agree or not, it took courage to come out against those who wage war for profit and caused the destabilization of Iraq in the first place. Especially when some of them might be on his team. (Of course, as it turned out, Iraq was overtaken by ISIS. But that would never have happened had the U.S. not needlessly started a war there.)

Glenn Beck's, apparently, sincere expression of patriotism gives me hope that he might be changing. Anyone can change and deserves the chance, and the right, to prove they can. If Beck is truly becoming more open-minded, with the power of his pulpit, he might help convince both conservatives and progressives to progress.

I've already written extensively, multiple times, about Patrick J. Buchanan's speaking out on issues, when he feels his team is wrong. Buchanan and, hopefully, Beck, realizes that life is not a sporting event. When you're right – you're right. And when you're wrong – you're wrong. It doesn't matter whose side you are (supposedly) on.

The biggest problem with free speech is that we sometimes forget what Noam Chomsky and the Supreme Court (although, not quite so eloquently) said about it. We want the right to free speech but, all too often, attempt to deny it to those who disagree with us, especially if their arguments prove us wrong. Why? (Come on, you know!) Because "it's absolutely threatening to admit you're wrong."

To use myself as an example, I refer you back to the open-letter I wrote to the CEO of American Airlines (Appendix B). Whether my "fellow employee" was management or rank-and-file, American Airlines was paying my bills, they were my team at the time. When I wrote that letter to the CEO, admonishing him for actions that were hurting the team, I was praised by everyone in my team-within-the-team, my union, including its leadership. But credit is due to that CEO as well, for considering one of his team-mate's criticism and making a policy change.

However, when things at American Airlines got "ugly," I wrote another letter that criticized the actions of my union. In it, I encouraged the work-force to protest and vote "NO" on the union's concessionary, Tentative Agreement with the company. Whatever motivated the union leadership to capitulate to concessions is not important at this time. What's important is that letter did not receive consideration from my team-mates – it got backfire. They forgot that to embrace free speech you must embrace the free speech of ideas you don't agree with. Rather than defend their motives and try to prove me wrong, which was what I wanted, they attacked my right to speak my mind because it was not in alignment with their beliefs. When we try to deny others the same (First Amendment) right we desire – everyone loses. (By the way, the outcome was that the Agreement was voted down, which prompted American Airlines to file bankruptcy and loot the workers anyway – with the help of the courts.)

Taking advantage of our right to free speech might be even more important when we disagree with our team-mates than it is when we disagree with the opposition.

"He who passively accepts evil is as much involved in it as he who helps to perpetrate it. He who accepts evil without protesting against it is really cooperating with it. "Dr. Martin Luther King, Jr.

To me, our most important Constitutional right, after freedom of speech, is also contained in the First Amendment – freedom of the press. That is because the free press is the guardian of the free flow of free speech, which is the foundation of any free society. And freedom of the press is becoming increasingly important because of the increasing prevalence of rapid technology as our main source of information. That is why we must be ever-vigilant in protecting the free press from, not only, infringement of its rights but also from abuse and misuse of its rights by the free press itself.

The rights of the free press are protected by the First Amendment. Occasionally, those rights still get violated. But the fact that law is in place to defend those rights makes them less attractive to violate and, if infringed upon, more difficult to violate effectively.

Abuse and misuse of its rights, by the free press itself, is a bit more difficult to control. And became even harder ever since 1987 when Ronald Reagan was successful in repealing the Fairness Doctrine, the regulation that guarded against it. Since then, any hooligan demagogue who wants to can be another Joe McCarthy or Herbert Hoover and call anyone: "Communist Revolutionaries" or "Fake News" or "SCUM" without offering one shred of evidence (as opposed to my demonstrating Ronald Reagan was a Communist by providing substantial evidence). Now, it's up to us to guard ourselves against the abuse of the right to freedom of the press.

But how do we guard against it? (Come on, you know!) First, don't just "trust a few sources more than others" (or, for that matter, any source) like a whopping 77% of Rush Limbaugh's audience said they do. Second, as writer Katherine Dunn said: Keeping good folks accountable doesn't imply they're bad folks. Be skeptical of both sides, even if one of them is your mother. Third, remember Judge Judy's advice: "Does it make sense?" And finally, fourth, remember what Dr. Mark Goulston teaches: "Think about what you're thinking." As I've said earlier:

As opposed to accepting 'facts' automatically, as offered by the first source we get them from, it is safer to be skeptical – even if (maybe especially if [?]) that source proclaims to side with our personal ideology.

Our rights to real, intellectual and emotional property, "Life, Liberty and the pursuit of Happiness," are the pillars our society was built upon. It is the first duty of government to protect those rights. And it's our duty to ensure that any government does that job. When a government fails to, we the people are entitled to the right of "legitimate revolution," as philosopher John Locke advised. We revolt by replacing the ineffective government through free elections.

But when we fail to protect all of our other rights, by not thinking about what we're thinking, we are easily led to act against our own best interests and elect a government that is even more ineffective. And even worse, a government that is only concerned with their interests – NOT OURS! That's when we feel frustrated, insecure, threatened and disturbed. Then, we stop listening and just hear (what we want to hear). And that's when we play "follow the leader." And around and around it goes.

Plutocrats and their loyal politicians and demagogues know this and cultivate it to control us. They cleverly use incendiary "Ideas about Ideas" like, abortion, healthcare, big (and small) government, religion and guns to keep us fighting amongst ourselves and disturbed. And they are constantly offering us scapegoats like (illegal) immigrants, "moochers" who hog all of our entitlements, and France, for us to fear and hate – to keep us insecure and threatened. Remember what reporter Joe Keohane discovered in researching his *Boston Globe* article "How Facts Backfire": The more strongly we feel about an issue the more motivated we are to hold on to it and the harder it is to change our minds. Additionally, the more insecure or threatened we feel the less likely we are to listen to dissenting opinions. This clarifies why demagogues keep people disturbed. The more fearful people are – the easier they are to manipulate. Then, all demagogues need do is convince us that their interests are commensurate with our interests.

Subversive Senator Joe McCarthy convinced us that his interests were commensurate with ours by claiming he would protect us against Communists and falsely accusing innocent Americans in order to prolong his sham – after – courting support from the American Communist Party to get elected. And we followed the leader.

Ronald Reagan did it by convincing us that he would protect the American worker and proceeded to attack and destroy as many work-place rights as he could. And we followed the leader – to this day!

Plutocrats created the Tea Party and convinced many sincere Conservatives that it was in their best interest to become extremists and support subversive politicians out to bankrupt the Government. And they followed the leader.

Why do we keep playing "follow the leader"? In addition to all the appeals to our emotions, demagoguery, propaganda and other persuasive arts being used to manipulate us there is one more phenomenon of psychology at play – "learned helplessness." And learned helplessness does not originate from outside forces, it emanates entirely from within us. It is the phenomenon of "giving up."

When injustice is overwhelming, people rarely rebel, they usually give up. Saul Alinsky

Psychologist Martin Seligman discovered the phenomenon of learned helplessness from experiments he did at the University of Pennsylvania in 1967. He found that when he subjected dogs to electrical shocks from which they had no escape they eventually quit trying to and acted as if helpless to change their predicament. When he later provided them with means of escape they still refused to try. That's learned helplessness.

How it applies to us was described by Martin Kaplan, Director of the Norman Lear Center and Professor at the USC Annenberg School, in an article he wrote, which was re-published in *The Huffington Post* on December 16, 2012: Learned helplessness is an affliction of our American essence that stems from our malfunctioning government. It's the sickening concession that we have no power to change what we want to change. It's the sad truth that the deck is stacked against us.

In the same article, Professor Kaplan added: Congress is populated with too many cowards, from both major parties; they protect their jobs ahead of protecting their fellow Americans. We know this! We hear it all the time! And because we feel helpless, we keep voting for cowards in the hope that one day they will change and protect *us* as they promise, instead of their jobs. THEY WON'T!

We are the ones who must change. We had hope for (Republican) Ronald Reagan but he betrayed us. We had hope for (Democrat) Barack Obama but he let us down. We (well, just enough of "we") had hope for "outsider" Donald Trump but ... oh boy! As long as we keep voting for politicians who are "married to the mob" nothing will change. It doesn't matter whether it's the Democratic mob or the Republican mob. They both answer to the same mob – the one with all the MONEY.

FOR GOD'S SAKE! For our sake – it's time to quit rooting for the same two teams, following the leader and acting helpless. It's time to stop thinking Right or Left, Conservative or Liberal and start thinking about our own common, best interests. It's time for all Americans to become radicals and "advocate thorough political reform" by having the courage to vote for Independent representatives and against mobbed-up politicians.

It's time to show the plutocrats who's the boss by enacting economic protest and hitting them in the wallet, where they feel pain.

It's time to exercise our right to "legitimate revolution" before it's too late!

XIV

Final Thoughts

"Change your thoughts and you change your world." Norman Vincent Peale

Time to wrap things up! As a fan of maxims and quotations, I want to end my study with some simple to remember words of wisdom from, well, the wise. Hopefully, these will help us keep things in proper perspective and help us remember what's important for us as Americans.

The first one is familiar to many and well known to anyone who has been to Alcoholics Anonymous or most any other twelve-step recovery group. I'm listing it at the beginning because if we can't get this one right none of the others can make any difference.

"God grant me the serenity to accept the things I cannot change, Courage to change the things I can change, And wisdom to know the difference."

That is, of course, AA's "Serenity Prayer." It's important because it teaches the *necessity* of change. The serenity to accept the things we cannot change is usually a snap. The wisdom to know the difference between those things and the things we can change is a little trickier but most of us can usually fake it, most often leaning toward "cannot change." The middle part, "courage to change the things I can change," is the hard one.

The Serenity Prayer is based on a prayer believed to have been written in 1937 by Reinhold Niebuhr: "Father, give us courage to change what must be altered, serenity to accept what cannot be helped, and the insight to know the one from the other."

Niebuhr, for those unfamiliar, was a great American theologian and has been credited by Dr. Martin Luther King, Jr., Senator John McCain and President Barack Obama, among others, as having influenced them. Niebuhr spoke out against racism and injustice. He supported Dr. King and opposed the Vietnam War. He criticized Henry Ford and aided workers in the struggle for better factory conditions. Niebuhr won the Presidential Medal of Freedom in 1964.

Reinhold Niebuhr was also a member of the American Socialist Party and a *true* anti-communist (Remember! They're – not – the – same!): "In the 1950s, Niebuhr described Senator Joseph McCarthy as a force of evil, not so much for attacking civil liberties, as for being ineffective in rooting out Communists and their sympathizers." (Fox, Richard/Reinhold Niebuhr/1985) Niebuhr denounced "utopianism" and wrote: "Man's capacity for justice makes democracy possible; but man's inclination to injustice makes democracy necessary." (Niebuhr, Reinhold/The Children of Light and the Children of Darkness/1944)

Reinhold Niebuhr had what he wrote about, "courage to change what must be altered."

Another great American who had the courage to do what needed to be done was Dr. Martin Luther King, Jr. He was a lot like my mother and father. That is, by his expression of many memorable quotations.

Dr. King gave one particular warning that we should heed now more than ever:

"Never forget that everything Hitler did in Germany was legal."

There is another caveat that needs to go right under that one, so I'll put it there:

"Those who cannot remember the past are condemned to repeat it."
George Santayana

If you want to refresh your memory as to why those two ideas are important to keep in mind *now,* re-read Chapter VIII, about the "philosophy" of plutocrats as taught by their Dear Sage, Ayn Rand.

Something plutocrats need to be reminded of relentlessly was written by Theodor Seuss Geisel:

"Even though you can't see or hear them at all, a person's a person, no matter how small." Dr. Seuss

As I said in one of my letters, the abusers of power might not believe that or even accept it. But we can certainly make them RESPECT it through the voting booth and economic protest. Run them out of town and hit them in the only place they feel pain – the wallet!

We can agree that we need change. We can summon the courage needed to make it happen. We can be inspired and even guided by leaders. However, nothing will change unless we get up and ACT in our own best interests.

"It is not in the stars to hold our destiny but in ourselves." William Shakespeare

"… the leader is us." Gavin Newsom

But before we can make change, we must change our mindset. So I will end with these few reminders about how to protect ourselves from being persuaded to act against our own best interests.

When Glenn Beck (or anyone else) says: "Don't take my word for it," "Have an open mind," or "Do your own homework," don't just consider doing it. DO IT, even if they don't say it! I did – for every page of this book.

After you've done your own homework – with an open mind – don't take anyone's word for it. Employ Judge Judy's advice and ask yourself: "Which side's arguments make the most sense?"

And *finally* finally, always remember what Dr. Mark Goulston teaches, which has been the theme I have based this book upon: "Think you know what I'm going to say?" Good! That means you're thinking about what you're thinking.

Thank you, God bless you and God bless America,
M.A.S. – September 2018

Afterthoughts

Thoughts about my thoughts

After thinking about what I've been writing – and thinking – I thought some of the things we've been thinking about should be thought about a little more. What the hell am I talking about?

Well, for instance, we talked about gullibility a lot. Science tells us how demagogues take advantage of the gullible as well as those simply not paying close enough attention. But I wondered: If science can tell us that, maybe it can also tell us why we are gullible in the first place? As it turns out – it can.

Remember what Tokyo Rose, I mean Ann Coulter, said? Propaganda is effective because most people are too busy and/or stupid to see it. People think they comprehend bias and recognize it, which is ridiculous. They surely don't. Unfortunately, she's right. But why?

What Coulter observes, described in her insulting and vulgar style, is the fact that we all use those mental shortcuts. Because most people are too busy (with other matters) – however, not necessarily stupid – we don't take the time to filter out the bias. The shortcut, it turns out, is the failure to employ the opposite of gullibility – skepticism.

In an online article he wrote for *Psychology Today,* clinical psychologist Leon F. Seltzer, Ph.D. explained that we fail to employ skepticism for a number of reasons, such as the need to impress, win acceptance or approval, or be "liked." (In other words, we want to feel like part of the team.) Another reason, the doctor pointed out, is the fear of admitting we do not comprehend what someone else is saying. (In other words, as said by Seltzer's colleague, Prof. Brendan Nyhan, "it's absolutely threatening to admit you're wrong.")

Dr. Seltzer defined gullibility as a weakness for being deceived, misled, and/or exploited – apart from intellect or societal competency. So in contradiction to Ann Coulter's hypothesis, gullibility has nothing to do with being stupid. In fact, the smartest among us can be the most gullible. Magician Ricky Jay said, in a *60 Minutes* interview, his (a magician's) perfect audience would be winners of the Nobel Prize because they often think they're too smart to be fooled. That's why they're the easiest people to fool.

When asked to explain our mental inclination toward gullibility in an online article for the science magazine *Discover,* developmental psychologist Stephen Greenspan, Ph.D., author of *Annals of Gullibility: Why We Get Duped and How to Avoid It* simply said: "People trust authority." (Remember how that was demonstrated, with chilling results, by the Milgram experiments?) And Dr. Leon F. Seltzer, in another of his online essays for *Psychology Today,* talked about how we develop that blind trust for authority. For most of us, it's a holdover from early childhood (because most of us didn't have psychologists for parents).

Before we learn the difference between right and wrong, we look for approval or acceptance from figures of authority that we trust. Those can be parents, teachers, other adults, older siblings or even peers we look up to. We do so in order to determine if our behavior is "okay."

When we are denied the approval or acceptance we seek we continue to seek it – even after we learn the difference between right and wrong, and even into adulthood. This phenomenon is what leads to the fact discovered by Dr. Stanley Milgram; few people have the ability to resist a figure of authority. We put undue trust in authority because we still don't trust ourselves enough.

The fact is that virtually all aspects of human society are based on trust. If we were all skeptical to the point of paranoia nothing would ever get done. Paul Hoffman, author of another *Discover* article, opined that it's quite sobering to think how blindly people trust authority figures when figures of authority such as Nobel Prize winners are the easiest people to fool.

Hoffman ended his article with a revelation that is, at the same time, both comforting and frightening, about the weakness toward gullibility that is wired into our brains. It turns out that Dr. Stephen Greenspan, author of *Annals of Gullibility* and considered the "authority's authority" on the subject, lost nearly half-a-million dollars of his personal retirement money because he "invested" it – with Bernie Madoff.

Speaking of brain-wiring, I've also been wondering if that's just an expression scientists use or an actual fact. Well, it turns out it's an actual fact.

Researchers at University College London, as well as other institutions, have done MRI studies of the brain activity in volunteers who described their philosophies as either conservative or liberal. It was found that the conservatives have larger and more active amygdalas. The amygdala is that part of the brain mainly concerned with emotion. Liberal brains have a larger and more active anterior cingulate cortex and more "gray matter." These components of the brain are involved in more complex thinking, such as learning and problem-solving.

Obviously, there's a joke in there, but it's not important now. What is important is the fact that our brain-wiring causes us to literally see the world differently. And the goal should be (for us) to find ways to overcome the differences. Some ways were discovered through studies at New York University.

Psychologist Jonathan Haidt of N.Y.U. remarked about how both conservative and liberal positions on provocative ideas (such as those we discussed in Chapter V) both emanate from personal moral values. Therefore, he suggested, rather than dismissing each other as immoral we should be seeking out our common values.

In research done at N.Y.U., the idea of global warming was represented to conservatives as being a threat to our American society, as opposed to being a crisis requiring management. Most conservatives don't even believe the idea of global warming is real. But after hearing the argument that environmental protection showed patriotism, an idea most conservatives firmly believe in, they were vastly more inclined to endorse it.

Of course, the argument can be made that the N.Y.U. researchers manipulated their subjects through language by employing flag-waving propaganda. And I would even agree they did, by appealing to their subjects' emotions. But remember, not all propaganda is bad. And since it was used to manipulate (which, although accurate, might be too harsh a word – persuade, I think, is more appropriate here) in order to help, not harm, the outcome of the propaganda was beneficial. That being, to encourage those with opposing views to find common values.

Given the right circumstances, and the right information, we can all find ways to come together. That is, if we remain open-minded. We can also drift further apart, if we do not.

I once heard Pulitzer Prize winning journalist, author and Presbyterian minister Chris Hedges remark that his job as a writer was "… to try and spread the truth insofar as I can determine it." And, he said, *our* job is "… to build movements that hold power accountable." My intention, with this book, was to do both. I hope that I was successful. But I know that I tried.

So to that end – while you think about what you're thinking – remember Bill O'Reilly's question: "Where do you stand?" I ask you to think about that, too.

Appendix A

A New Approach to Guns?

Two things have finally made it apparent, to me, why despite repeated mass killings, we have been unable to enact safer gun laws: (1) Congressman Steve Scalise, who was shot by a madman, said in interviews that his stance AGAINST gun control laws has not changed. He added that; stricter gun control would have prevented his being saved from his attacker. It doesn't seem important to him that his saviors were "police." (2) The Las Vegas mass shooter/killer owned over 60 legal guns (SIXTY GUNS!) and he kept them in his home (IN HIS HOME!). These two things exemplify why we have failed to improve gun safety laws because they demonstrate that our approach has always been counterintuitive. When politicians are so blinded by greed they can be shot (themselves) and still kowtow to the NRA and gun makers, there's something wrong with the opposing argument.

The NRA will not stop giving massive contributions to politicians on behalf of the gun makers. Gun makers will not stop demanding laws that allow anyone to own any and all guns they want. Therefore: "If you can't beat them – join them!"

If gun makers are allowed to sell all the guns they want they will be happy. So let them. If gun lovers are allowed to own all the guns they want they will be happy. So let them. BUT! Why not find ways to make everyone safer and (here's the key to get the NRA, gun makers and politicians on-board) let everyone make even more money at the same time?

There is no rational reason to have sixty guns in your house. If you want to own that many guns, fine. But require all except a few for home protection (say, one shotgun, one rifle and, if you qualify, one handgun) be kept in gun repositories. The gun repositories will allow anyone to own any, and many, guns and keep everyone safer in the process. Furthermore, they will put empty buildings back to good use, create jobs, and add to state and federal income. Why should the DMV be the only breadwinner?

Additionally, require every gun to have an annual registration sticker, just like a car. Anyone caught with an unregistered gun gets a fine; second offense, lose that gun; third offense, lose your license to own guns; etc. Let private enterprise, like the gun makers and the NRA, run the licensing bureaus and repositories and get a share of the profits. But let the workers be government employees, like the Post Office.

The politicians, gun makers and NRA will never support reducing the number of guns, which will reduce profits. But convincing them that they can vastly increase profits, by expanding their efforts to gun management and safety, might be the way to (FINALLY) win them over. Once they smell the dough they will figure out how to convince the gun owners of the plan's merits.

Appendix B

<u>An Open Letter to Gerard J. Arpey – Chief Executive Officer, American Airlines</u>:

Dear Fellow Employee;

The other day, I received your letter of thanks, for my hard work, which helped us achieve a $317 million profit this past fiscal quarter. As you see, I have begun this letter with the same salutation you used in yours. I want you to know that, as your fellow employee, I too feel that we must continue "Working Together" for our mutual future. I also want to thank you, for your hard work, and I say that with total honesty. I appreciate, from the dealings I have had with you and other AA executives, while I served as a Transport Workers Union Representative, how hard you work, and that you deserve to be rewarded for it – as we all do!

There is a current television commercial, for a well-known credit card company, which addresses the subject of <u>rewards</u>. In it, a medieval knight rides into town and proclaims: "I've slain the dragon! I've saved the village!" As his "reward," the king presents him with a thank you card. The knight, who is understandably disappointed and dejected, asks; "Is this all I get?" Then, the king proceeds to read a list of stipulations, on how many dragons must be slain and how many other heroic feats must be accomplished, before any "tangible reward" will be given. (Here comes the cute kicker!) How many dragons do I need to slay before I get a "tangible reward"?

In all seriousness and with all sincerity, I am beginning to wonder if you appreciate, or even realize, how disappointed and dejected your fellow employees are. Several days before I got your "thank you card," I read in the news that you (executives) "awarded yourselves" more stock options, payable in 2010. After the extensive criticism you received over the last options in April, that announcement, without any mention of some kind of compensation (even being considered) for the rest of the workforce, was astonishing. Your "thank you card," right on its heels was, at best, thoughtless. It almost seems like American Airlines is purposely undoing all the hard work we have accomplished, and you begged for, in turning the company around.

You may be wondering why I did not bring my concerns to you directly and have chosen instead to "air our laundry in public." I have several reasons. Primarily, I want to try to get your attention. I have conferred with my Union leaders and with the consultants hired by the company, to facilitate the "Turn-Around Plan," they all assured me that they spoke up and gave suggestions on how to handle the executive pay more amicably, for everyone; they did not get your attention. When the executive stock options were paid in April, a petition with 17,000 signatures, of employees, customers, and former customers, was e-mailed to all of you, calling for some kind of consideration for the rest of the workforce; it did not get your attention. At the annual Stockholders Meeting in April, hardbound copies of the petition were presented to, and ignored by, you and the Board of Directors. Many comments and concerns about the lack of equity shown to the AA labor force were voiced at the same meeting. Granted, some were inappropriate, but most were legitimate; none of that got your attention. In fact, I attended the Stockholders Meeting, and I was fascinated by your "non-positional" position, on every controversial remark. I have seen that before and since; your management team appears to like the approach that if you pretend a problem does not exist, it will go away. Consider however; the "problem" here is an unappreciated and unhappy workforce, if it goes away, there will be no AA.

Secondly, I want to try to get other people's attention. If my action of presenting this open letter, in a public forum, motivates others to action; maybe that will get your attention.

Thirdly, others who are not part of the "AA Family" are already speaking up about us, in the mainstream media. The business section of my local newspaper ran an article that excoriated you for the announcement of the 2010 executive stock options. In it, the reporter made several suggestions, as to how you might include "rewards" for the rest of the workforce. He opined that: "It would remind everyone that the troops eat before the generals." Additionally, he said, "it would give American managers some moral authority."

He went on to question if you were "holding back" until contract negotiations resume, so that you can ask for more concessions and in turn "reward" us with what we have already "earned." "But," he added, "imagine if employees took the same approach. What if they refuse to go the extra mile until new contracts are worked out next year?" That question worried me, and ought to worry you. I am worried that more (business) reporters and (industry) analysts will ask those kinds of questions, in newspaper and broadcast venues. If enough of them do, <u>more</u> of the public could become <u>former</u> customers.

Herb Cohen, the renowned negotiator and author, teaches, "perception is reality." If the public perceives that, by flying on American Airlines, they will be taking a chance, of getting sub par service, of having their luggage mishandled, or of their flight having a long delay, if it gets off the ground at all, et cetera, none of those things needs to happen. The public's perception will cause them to take their business elsewhere.

As your fellow employee, when your actions are detrimental to our mutual future, it is my responsibility <u>to get your attention</u> and make you aware of it. That is my straightforward, and only, purpose for this letter. Your actions are demoralizing the workforce – and creating doubts about our productivity, to outside observers. These are not imaginings; they are facts, and should be of concern to all of us, while all is not yet lost. In the newspaper article, I have been quoting, the reporter also stated: "It's always the right time to do the right thing - that's what leadership is about."

The credit card company, which I mentioned earlier, ends all of their commercials with the same catch-phrase question: "What's in your wallet?" No one needs to ask that question of you, it is public knowledge. However, the public and I need to worry about what's in ours.

Yours truly,
Michael A. Serrapica – American Airlines Employee, Transport Workers Union Member

Appendix C

Horton Hears a Coup: Reflections on AMR's Bankruptcy

After AMR's leaders have heard they have not been fair or honest repeatedly, by rewarding themselves and not sharing with their workers, as they promised to in negotiated contracts, they decided to stage a coup. They pushed out those at the top who protested, installed Mr. Tom Horton as their stooge CEO, and declared bankruptcy. AMR has over $4 Billion in reserve cash, but corporate bankruptcy laws allow corporations to declare bankruptcy when they aren't actually bankrupt. Does that make sense?

Many of us have lost pay, benefits, and pensions because we've worked for companies that have staged coups. But the thought of losing what we have, even though it's less, makes us fear rocking the boat. The time has come to capsize the boat and stage a counter-coup!

From the standpoint of the people, whether or not we work for AMR, this company's bankruptcy provides a golden opportunity to say enough is enough. AMR Corporation can be made the poster child for corporate greed, as well as the example of how to fight it. In the Dr. Seuss book that inspired this article's title – *Horton Hears a Who!* – the title character continually reinforces the moral of the story, which is: "*Even though you can't see or hear them at all, a person's a person, no matter how small.*" We may not be able to make the profiteers at AMR, or any other corporation, believe that or even accept it. However, we absolutely can make them RESPECT it!

Might it get AMR's attention if they knew that on a regular basis hundreds of "non-buying shoppers" will show up at American Airlines' ticket counters, at all their major airports, and occupy the agents with questions about flights, which they will never take? Do you think something like that, and similar (perfectly legal) actions, may just convince AMR to be more humble and less greedy when they walk into the bankruptcy court? If now is not the time to employ aggressive strategies when will it be? AMR's workers already know that our employer's intention is to legally loot us. We have the organizing capability in the hands of our labor leaders. We have an enormous army. At this fortunate point in history we even have reserve troops who are both motivated and willing to help, they call themselves "The Occupy Movement." And, most important of all, we have the motivation – survival.

In an article written by TWU International President, James C. Little, about the AMR bankruptcy, he said: *"This failure by both business and government makes you want to go out and 'occupy' something."* We now have our chance to back him up. All workers, union and non-union, not only at AMR but everywhere, should be contacting our Local Union Representatives, civic leaders, the AFL-CIO, and people like President Little. We need to encourage them to pressure the morally bankrupt leaders of AMR, who no longer listen to words of protest. We need to use AMR as an example that other, would-be robber barons will fear, by hitting them in the only place they feel pain, the wallet!

Michael A. Serrapica,
TWU Member - AMR Worker

Appendix D

Long Forgotten Legacy of Freedom
by
Michael A. Serrapica (TWU Member)

On Memorial Day 2006, Public Television Stations aired a documentary called *The March of The Bonus Army*. It chronicled a very little known saga in our nation's history, which was also so important that it changed our country in many ways and for all time.

During World War I, for the first time in history, the American Military was made up of a majority of draftees. The Selective Service Act accomplished this. Most went to fight in combat "over there." But some were selected to work in war related industries or as farmers "over here." Those who served at home earned, on average, ten times what was paid to combat soldiers. After the war, those who served in combat asked the government for back wages, to make up for the earnings they lost while fighting for our freedom. They referred to it as Adjusted Compensation. Their detractors called it a bonus.

In 1924, Congress granted World War I veterans "Adjusted Universal Compensation" of approximately $1.00 to $1.25 per day of service. It was to be paid either upon death or in the year 1945, whichever came first. That stipulation earned the Congressional grant an unflattering nickname: The Tombstone Bonus.

After the onset of The Great Depression, a bill was introduced in Congress to pay "the bonus" immediately. As veterans followed the dealings of Congress in the newspapers, they fumed as their bill stagnated, while big business profited from Congressional grants. The fuse, which sparked the march of "The Bonus Army," had finally been ignited.

It began with 300 unemployed veterans from Portland, Oregon. When they set out they had, in total, $30.00 to their name. They hopped trains, hitched rides and marched toward Washington D.C., in 1932. As word of the march spread their ranks began to swell with groups and individuals from coast to coast. Entire families, husbands, wives and children together, joined. If they had transportation they took advantage of it, if they did not they marched. There was nothing else for them to do; they were out of work, out of food and out of money. But they were not out of hope or determination. The Bonus Army was also integrated, something considered provocative and dangerous at the time and, in certain instances, still is.

As they arrived in Washington, The Bonus Army began to organize. They set up encampments, the largest one at a vacant area just outside of downtown Washington D.C., called Anacostia. They elected leaders and devised their battle plans. Some were lucky enough to find part-time work, but for the most part they existed on the charity of individuals or organizations like The Salvation Army. At the height of their strength The Bonus Army numbered 45,000.

The Attack is Launched

Throughout the spring and summer of 1932 The Bonus Army marched and paraded on the streets of Washington D.C. They lobbied Congressional Representatives. They camped out, inside and outside of the buildings where members of Congress had offices. They became a big, collective, but peaceful and legal, pain in the neck. After just two weeks they won a victory; the Bonus Bill was passed in The House of Representatives.

On June 17 the Bonus Bill went to the Senate. To pressure Senators to vote affirmatively The Bonus Army began a vigil on Capitol Hill. They sang, to the tune of "Over There," *"Over Here – Over Here... The Yanks are starving,"* and could be heard inside the Senate chambers. At the end of the day the bill was defeated, overwhelmingly. The heartbroken veterans sang "America" and disbursed peacefully.

One month later, on July 16, the last day of the Congressional session, the once again resolved veterans surrounded the Capitol Building. Congress members snuck out through tunnels and back doors. President Hoover ordered the active Army to evict The Bonus Army from downtown Washington D.C.

The Counter Attack

By this time many of The Bonus Army marchers had gone home, but over 11,500 men, women and children remained in Washington. Many stayed because they simply had no home to go to. On July 28 the eviction began, at first by the Washington D.C. Police. Trouble started and so did bloodshed. Some policemen were hit with rocks and a couple fired their guns; two veterans were killed. Then, the Army was sent in.

Three men, who would become famous during World War II, led the troops. One was Dwight Eisenhower, one was George S. Patton, but the Commander that day was Douglas MacArthur. At 4:30 PM, MacArthur ordered The United States Army to attack the unarmed men, women and children of The Bonus Army, with tanks, tear gas and rifles with affixed bayonets. They pushed The Bonus Army out of downtown Washington and across the bridge that led to their camp at Anacostia. Around midnight, MacArthur did something that would become one of his trademarks and ultimately led to his being fired, by President Truman; he disobeyed orders. President Hoover specified that the veterans were to be evacuated from downtown Washington and that (U.S. Army) troops were not to cross the bridge. MacArthur defiantly ordered his troops to cross into Camp Anacostia and burn it to the ground. They set fire to every shack and tent, as well as the American flags that flew from every hovel. The next day public opinion began to turn against President Hoover, after he called the veterans "Communist Revolutionaries" without offering one shred of evidence.

In November, Hoover lost the election to Franklin Delano Roosevelt. But FDR was also unsupportive of the Bonus Bill. Veterans continued to march on Washington, in smaller groups, every year. Roosevelt knew he could not use force against them again, but he still wanted to keep them out of Washington D.C. He had many sent to work in "rehabilitation camps" in the Florida Keys. On September 2, 1935, Labor Day, several hundred veterans were killed by the most powerful hurricane to ever hit the United States, in history. The government tried to cover up the blunders and negligence that left them exposed. But one of the first people to get to the area after the tragedy was author and journalist Earnest Hemingway, a Keys resident.

Hemingway wrote a scathing article about the horrors he saw and how government ineptitude left the veterans to face the hurricane unprotected. He wrote of the veteran's bodies that were found on the beach, which had been blasted by the wind-ravaged sand; literally skinned alive. Opposition to paying the bonus finally began to change. In 1936 the Bonus Bill passed both Houses of Congress but was again vetoed by FDR, for the fourth time. Congress voted to override the President's veto and four million World War I Veterans got their back pay at last.

The Legacy

In 1944 FDR signed The G.I. Bill of Rights into law, guaranteeing that all veterans would henceforth be compensated for their losses during time served in the military. The G.I. Bill also gave veterans the opportunities to get an education, afford a home and start a business. The G.I. Bill changed America.

The Bonus Army changed America. Every G.I. now takes for granted that the government will keep its promises, thanks to The Bonus Army. Ever since 1932 every group that has peacefully and legally marched on Washington D.C. has had a model to base itself on, thanks to The Bonus Army. Labor unions can cite The Bonus Army as an example of how a common cause can unite a mass of individuals into a powerful and unyielding force. Will we ever again see a group quite as diligent and determined as The Bonus Army was? Not until another group has nothing left to lose; as long as we all have just enough to keep us quiet we probably will not.

*Notes:

1. This article is based on *The March of The Bonus Army* (Public Broadcasting Service, 2006) and *The Bonus Army, An American Epic* by Paul Dickson and Thomas B. Allen (New York: Walker & Company, 2004)

2. The author's father, Antonio M. Serrapica (1901-1986), was a proud veteran of The United States Navy (World War I); The United States Army and Merchant Marines (World War II); and of The Bonus Army (1932).

About The Author

Michael Serrapica was born in New York City and grew up in The Bronx. He graduated from Aviation High School in Queens, New York with a vocational diploma and Federal Aviation Administration Airframe and Powerplant Mechanic Licenses. His career in aviation spanned 33 years with 2 major airlines in 3 major cities.

Although foregoing formal university, Mr. Serrapica has a diverse background of private school, as well as personal and experiential education in several fields. He has studied acting, advertising, broadcasting, marketing and radio and television performance and production at private schools in New York City. He studied management at Sears Roebuck and Company. He studied arbitration at The National Labor College in Maryland. He has worked as an actor and announcer in radio, television and film. During his airline career he served as a Shop Steward for the International Association of Machinists, and Local Vice-President and International Media Representative for the Transport Workers Union of America. He has also been, and still is, an activist, demonstrator and protester.

Mr. Serrapica's knowledge and experience has given him a keen awareness of the power of the various methods of persuasion. By writing *Conned Conservatives and Led-on Liberals* he undertook a personal journey to understand how those methods are used to entice non-experts (like him) into acting against their own best interests. In his book he shares what he learned from "the experts," peer-to-peer, so that he (and you) can avoid being *conned* or *led-on*.

Made in the USA
Columbia, SC
10 March 2019